Your

CALIFORNIA

WILLS, TRUSTS, & ESTATES
EXPLAINED SIMPLY:

Important Information You Need to Know for California Residents

By Linda C. Ashar, Attorney at Law

YOUR CALIFORNIA WILLS, TRUSTS, & ESTATES EXPLAINED SIMPLY: IMPORTANT INFORMATION YOU NEED TO KNOW FOR CALIFORNIA RESIDENTS

Copyright © 2015 Atlantic Publishing Group, Inc.
1405 SW 6th Avenue • Ocala, Florida 34471 • Phone 800-814-1132 • Fax 352-622-1875
Website: www.atlantic-pub.com • E-mail: sales@atlantic-pub.com
SAN Number: 268-1250

Library of Congress Cataloging-in-Publication Data

Ashar, Linda C., 1947-
  Your California wills, trusts, & estates explained simply : important information you need to know for California residents / by Linda C. Ashar.
    p. cm.
  Includes bibliographical references and index.
  ISBN-13: 978-1-60138-410-2 (alk. paper)
  ISBN-10: 1-60138-410-6 (alk. paper)
  1. Estate planning--California--Popular works. 2. Inheritance and succession--California--Popular works. I. Title. II. Title: Your California wills, trusts, and estates explained simply.
  KFC195.A98 2010
  332.024'01609794--dc22
                    2010027187

Printed in the United States

Printed on Recycled Paper

A few years back we lost our beloved pet dog Bear, who was not only our best and dearest friend but also the "Vice President of Sunshine" here at Atlantic Publishing. He did not receive a salary but worked tirelessly 24 hours a day to please his parents.

Bear was a rescue dog who turned around and showered myself, my wife, Sherri, his grandparents Jean, Bob, and Nancy, and every person and animal he met (well, maybe not rabbits) with friendship and love. He made a lot of people smile every day.

We wanted you to know a portion of the profits of this book will be donated in Bear's memory to local animal shelters, parks, conservation organizations, and other individuals and nonprofit organizations in need of assistance.

– *Douglas & Sherri Brown*

PS: We have since adopted two more rescue dogs: first Scout, and the following year, Ginger. They were both mixed golden retrievers who needed a home.

Want to help animals and the world? Here are a dozen easy suggestions you and your family can implement today:

- *Adopt and rescue a pet from a local shelter.*
- *Support local and no-kill animal shelters.*
- *Plant a tree to honor someone you love.*
- *Be a developer — put up some birdhouses.*
- *Buy live, potted Christmas trees and replant them.*
- *Make sure you spend time with your animals each day.*
- *Save natural resources by recycling and buying recycled products.*
- *Drink tap water, or filter your own water at home.*
- *Whenever possible, limit your use of or do not use pesticides.*
- *If you eat seafood, make sustainable choices.*
- *Support your local farmers market.*
- *Get outside. Visit a park, volunteer, walk your dog, or ride your bike.*

Five years ago, Atlantic Publishing signed the Green Press Initiative. These guidelines promote environmentally friendly practices, such as using recycled stock and vegetable-based inks, avoiding waste, choosing energy-efficient resources, and promoting a no-pulping policy. We now use 100-percent recycled stock on all our books. The results: in one year, switching to post-consumer recycled stock saved 24 mature trees, 5,000 gallons of water, the equivalent of the total energy used for one home in a year, and the equivalent of the greenhouse gases from one car driven for a year.

DEDICATION

To my family. — Linda C. Ashar, attorney at law

BIOGRAPHY

Linda C. Ashar is a lawyer, educator, horse breeder, freelance writer, and artist. She has practiced law for more than 25 years before the Ohio and Federal Bars. She is a senior shareholder in the firm of Wickens, Herzer, Panza, Cook, & Batista Co. in Avon, Ohio. In addition to her Juris Doctor in law, she holds a Master of Arts in special education and a Bachelor of Arts in English.

She is a professional writer and has authored *101 Ways to Score Higher on Your LSAT: What You Need to Know About the Law School Admission Test Explained Simply, The Complete Power of Attorney Guide for Consumers* and *Small Businesses: Everything You Need to Know Explained Simply,* an estate planning book series with Atlantic Publishing Group, poetry, and several magazine and journal articles, including a collection on Suite101.com. She is an adjunct professor at DeVry University and Keller Graduate School and a frequent speaker at law seminars. Reach her at ashar@hbr.net or lashar@wickenslaw.com.

TABLE OF CONTENTS

Chapter 8: Retirement Accounts 141

Chapter 9: Setting Priorities 157

Chapter 10: Choosing Who, What, How, When, and Why 171

Chapter 11: Planning Your Estate: Last Will and Testament in California 185

INTRODUCTION
Estate Planning: What Is It?

Many estate-planning books suggest you begin the process by taking inventory of all the possessions you will leave behind. This does make a certain amount of sense because disposing of these things according to your wishes is a part of estate planning. The problem is you could end up with an extremely long list that includes every CD you own, not to mention the entire contents of your junk drawer. You might have some idea of what matters to you now, but what about five months or 50 years from now?

Asking difficult questions and understanding your priorities are the two most important parts of estate planning. Whether you need a trust, additional life insurance, or a living will depends on what you want, not what a lawyer or an accountant tells you to do. Making such choices, though, can be difficult. *The first three chapters in this book are designed help you focus on the process of determining what you want.*

Once you have a sense of the elements of estate planning that are important to you, you have a reason to dig into the details of wills, beneficiaries, taxes, and all that other minutiae related to planning for whom you, not the courts or governments, want to benefit from your lifetime of hard work.

In this book, we provide a common-sense philosophy and approach to estate planning to give you a place to start. The first part of the book outlines broadly applicable principles. The laws of your state control several aspects of estate planning and provisions for your property. *In Chapter 11, we focus on the specific requirements for California residents.*

Throughout this book, you will see checklists, tip boxes, and case studies by professionals or people in your similar situation to help you with the process of planning your estate. *Worksheets are provided in Appendix A.*

None of the information provided in this book is intended to be or should be interpreted as legal advice. Each person's situation is different and depends on specific facts and circumstances. For legal advice specific to your situation, seek legal counsel from an attorney in your state who is trained or experienced in the field of estate planning and trusts.

Yosemite valley from tunnel view, Yosemite National Park, California, USA

CHAPTER 1
Getting Started

"Men in my family live well into their 70s, so I have plenty of time to do this."

"I created a will when my children were born. They are the only valuable 'possessions' I have, and they are already taken care of."

"This is only my third year in a full-time job. I have student loans to pay off and make no money. I do not have an estate to plan."

"We have been married for 12 years. If one of us dies before we get around to our estate planning, the spouse inherits everything; everyone knows that."

"Estate planning is for old people."

"I'll think about it tomorrow."

These typical reasons for not estate planning are as varied and creative as the reasons children who did not do their homework concot. But unlike a teacher, who can excuse a missing paper, the state — the government body ultimately responsible for resolving all legal matters related to anything a person who died left behind — does not accept excuses from the next of kin — spouse, child, parents, or otherwise.

State statutes tell a judge how to distribute real estate; pay credit card debts; satisfy mortgages; and assign cash, grandma's antique end table, and the boxes of personal papers stashed in the attic. To make matters more confusing, each state has at least a slightly different idea about how to handle the process, and Congress keeps changing the tax rules at the federal level.

According to estate-planning professionals, all the typical explanations for putting off estate planning are excuses for avoiding two of the most taboo subjects in many cultures: money and death. With death comes feelings of fear, denial, and anger. With money comes issues with self-worth, concern about the perceptions of others, and worry about the ability to support those who need help. These feelings and issues combine to create an emotional quagmire.

Pile on top of all that the unfamiliar terminology, complicated tax laws, and a host of people who have their hands out for a chunk of your estate, and planning for what happens after your death is enough to cause anyone to exclaim, "The dog ate my estate plan!"

Estate Planning Simplified

As with all complicated tasks, the best way to begin is to deal with individual pieces of information.

In simple terms, estate planning is creating a set of instructions about what should be done before and after you die with your assets and personal belongings, including money, possessions, investments, collectibles, and anything else you own. It is more than writing a will that distributes your best china and savings accounts or a to-do list of things you want done and bills that must be paid. It is more than finding a good asking price for your house or someone to take care of your collie, Fluffy.

Anyone who has possessions, no matter how many or few, needs to plan his or her estate. After you die, the mortgage payment still must be made, and your favorite charity is still going to need the new roof or donation you pledged, but you will not be there to write the checks. The bank and the charity will express sympathy to your family, but they will be looking for the benefit of their commitment. Your family will not know how you want things handled if you have not left instructions, and they will not be bound to follow your wishes if you have not sealed them into legal documents.

This thing called estate planning is just a continuation of what you do now: sharing yourself, your money, and your life experiences with the people and organizations that are important to you. Estate planning allows you to make sure the money and property you accumulated during your life can continue to serve your purposes after you can no longer direct matters yourself.

You can do some things with your estate before you die, but there are some steps that cannot be taken until your death. Consider technical aspects, such as paying taxes and distributing your belongings. Before you can get to any of those details, you need to understand where you are in your life and the fact it will end at some point.

Everyone Dies: A Simple Statement with Complicated Implications

Some people embrace a belief or philosophy that perceives death as a new adventure — the next step in living. Most people, though, do not see death, or even thinking about it, as fun or exciting. Dying and all the trappings related to it rarely come up at the dinner table between "Pass the green beans," and "What's for dessert?" Given a choice between a conversation about death and clearing the dishes, people will fall over each other to head for the kitchen.

The less death is discussed, the more taboo it becomes and the more uncomfortable people feel when it does come up. Avoiding the subject of death and those who are left behind only makes it a frightening topic. As with learning mathematical equations or the periodic table of elements in chemistry, practice and repetition can demystify the unknown and put it in a more calming perspective.

Numerous books cover death and dying. As these books have increased in number and popularity, some basic knowledge has crept into everyday language and consciousness. Dr. Elisabeth Kübler-Ross, who wrote *On Death and Dying*, mainstreamed the acceptance of grief as a reasonable, human emotion. She used grief, the sad, gut-wrenching feeling over losing someone loved or something cherished, to create a list of the emotional stages people experience when faced with a profound loss. These stages of grief have come to be embraced and recognized as normal and necessary in the human experience.

The Five Stages of Grief

1. **Denial and isolation:** disbelieving the loss has taken place and possibly withdrawing from   family routines and people

2. **Anger:** feeling furious at the person who inflicted the hurt or at the world for letting it happen or upset with oneself for allowing the loss to occur, even if nothing could have stopped it

3. **Bargaining:** attempting to negotiate with a higher power for a different outcome or miraculous solution

4. **Depression:** feeling numb, lost, and unhappy and possibly still angry and sad

5. **Acceptance:** calming, maybe even fading, of unsettling feelings and finally acknowledging the reality of the loss

Even just imagining the loss of a loved one or one's own death can give rise to a semblance of these feelings. The advantage of facing these emotions is the opportunity to face any self-doubt, fears, and anxiety that otherwise lurk undetected or beneath the events of daily living.

Contemplating the inevitability of mortality does not need to be all negative. You can also use the process for thinking about the accomplishments, successes, and positive impacts you have had and expect to have yet. The estate-planning process can enable you to develop a more realistic view of yourself, your values, and the fruits of your efforts. The act of planning empowers you to overcome any fears and worries about a seemingly dreary subject matter. You can also begin to see the fruits of your labor have meaning and direction for you now.

Money Talk

Most adults do not want to include children in discussions of financial issues because they see it as a burden or a scary subject for their children. However, without age-appropriate participation in conversations about family finances, children will never learn about the role and impact of money. An exclusionary approach turns money into an off-limits topic. It can also make money appear to be the cause of problems, a bad thing, or even a big secret.

By taking time to consider your past experiences with money, you can begin to understand the source of negative feelings or worries. You can also clarify the importance money has in your life. Decisions about the future are going to be difficult at best if you do not know what you want to accomplish and disastrous if you make choices that are at odds with your true hopes and dreams or are unrealistic for your circumstances.

One strong influence that can lead to misguided financial decisions is what other people can afford. Even if you do not think about painting your house to make it look as good as your neighbor's house that was just repainted, you most likely notice who has just repainted their house, who has a new car, and who is going on vacation. The amount of disposable income someone has can create a materialistic link between net worth and self-worth.

A benefit of estate planning is getting a realistic grasp on your present circumstances and a developing concrete plan for the future.

I Do What with All This?

The point of giving serious thought to death and money is to sort through the mental and physical obstacles that cause you to put off planning your estate.

To avoid feeling overwhelmed, or perhaps to feel you are accomplishing something, consider using a practical, logical method for collecting and organizing potentially emotional and volatile memories, experiences, and thoughts and basic preliminary documents.

Lists

Consider the topics that relate to you and your life situation; some suggestions are presented for you below. Create a list for each topic and organize the content into groups based on a common thread. Consider all possible angles, including past, present, and future, for every topic. Be honest. Nobody needs to see your lists but you. For example:

Money

Childhood and family memories

- Hearing mom and dad argue about the mortgage at the end of every month
- Getting a piggy bank from grandma and money every birthday to save for college
- Handing the bank teller a savings book and a bag of pennies, and getting a smile and a sucker
- Having a Christmas bank account
- Earning an allowance and giving part of it to the family church, synagogue, or favorite charity

Adolescent memories

- Running a lemonade stand as a Saturday afternoon project with friends, figuring out how to pay for ingredients and cups, setting the price, and splitting the profits — making my first dollar
- Being the only one who did not go on the class trip to Washington, D.C., because dad was just laid off
- Working a summer job at a local grocery store

Adult experiences

- Having no money to tow my first car when it died on the freeway
- Getting that first student loan payment book after graduation
- Photocopying my first paycheck
- Overdrawing my checking account
- Paying my own rent and bills and having money left to send home

Dreams

- Owning my own home
- Paying for in-home care for mom and dad

- Having three children and sending them all to college
- Spending a year abroad before I die
- Not having to worry about paying bills every month
- Having enough capital to start my own business

Career versus job

Childhood and family memories

- Receiving lectures on work ethic from grandpa while cleaning out the garage
- Hearing grandma telling me to put work off and have fun
- Having an uncle who lived with us and never seemed to have a job
- Having two parents who worked

Adolescent memories

- Working hard to raise money for school through a summer car wash
- Receiving advice from a career counselor at school who insisted my test scores meant I was going to be an engineer
- Wanting to dance in the school musical
- Quitting marching band to play football

Adult experiences

- Trying to make a hobby of skateboarding into a business
- Intensely disliking orders from boss who micromanaged
- Feeling terrorized by bills
- Witnessing corporate downsizing

Dreams

- Having a job to make money to support the rest of my life
- Not owning so many items I need a storage locker to hold them

- Having a job that allows me to support and spend time with a family
- Retiring at 50

Other topics to focus on include death, family, career, playtime and recreation, fears and worries, and anything else that evokes strong emotions as you consider other issues.

Journal

Choose a book with blank pages in which to record your estate-planning experience. Create sections for various stages of the process and leave room for facts and figures, your feelings, and your thoughts. Leave space for doodles, notes, and questions. Have pages for free association. For example, write "money" at the top of a page and write down what immediately comes to mind.

Stuff box

Find an old shoebox, or go out and buy something special for the estate-planning occasion. Put in your lists, napkins with thoughts you scribbled on them while drinking coffee, and your journal. This gives you a dedicated place for all the planning bits and pieces and documents in any form when you need them. If a movie ticket stub reminds you of the film documentaries you want to make someday, toss it in.

File folders

If you need more structure in your life, create a folder each time you address a specific topic, including the topic of preparing for estate planning. Choose family photos or pictures from a magazine that illustrate what matters most to you, and tape or staple one into each folder. When you get frustrated or annoyed, look at those pictures to remind yourself of the reason the work is necessary.

Use index cards to jot down thoughts, or digitally record them while you commute to and from work or sit outside by yourself on the porch, patio, yard, or beach. The method does not matter; the work is what counts. Once you identify the factors that prevent you from planning for your death, you will be able to more clearly use the present to help guide the future.

Here and Now

Beyond the complex emotions related to death and money, you need to figure out what is most important to you so you can set some goals for what you want to happen after you die. How to go about doing that effectively depends on the individual and other people involved.

How one spouse views money can be dramatically different from the other spouse's viewpoint. The people and things you each value might differ as well. What is valuable can be difficult to define because of the way culture places high importance on materialistic things. Creating a personal values list is one way to begin identifying what matters most to you.

For example, some people might choose family. Things necessary to survive, such as food, water, shelter, and medical care, are important but do not represent a value you hold. To distinguish these points, consider the following definitions:

- **Need:** a requirement; a necessity
- **Want:** something desired deeply or wished for
- **Value:** something held in high regard, appreciated and rated highly; a moral view

Once you can distinguish your needs, wants, and values, consider the role values play in your daily life. What you value tends to serve as the test or measuring stick for making decisions. When planning a summer vacation, do you feel it is more important to get away from daily stresses and relax in quiet with your immediate family, or is going on vacation without your parents and siblings never an option? Do you make sure you never miss events, such as weddings and graduations, with your extended family? You might value your extended family as much as you value your immediate family, or your immediate family might be the foremost consideration in all decision making. No one of these views is the only right one. What is important is to understand which view is yours.

Stepping out of your everyday life to thoughtfully consider what makes up your everyday life is a way to gain perspective on what matters to you. Here are some matters to consider:

You

- Are you postponing something now, such as learning to paint, because you feel something else is more important, such as tutoring for your children?
- Are you a spiritual or religious person?
- Do you want your children to have everything you did not?
- Is your decision making impulsive or thoughtful?
- Do you have time every day to do something you want to do? If not, why not?

Family

- How many children do you have or want to have? If you have children, is possible you will have more some day, either by birth or adoption?
- What if infertility becomes an issue? Do you want to adopt or consider other options?
- Are you close to your parents? Siblings? Other relatives?
- Which role does extended family play in your life?
- Are there any relatives with whom you are particularly close?
- Are there relatives with whom you are estranged?
- Are there any family members who are missing?

- Do you have children from a former marriage?
- Have you parented a child or children outside of legally recognized marriage?

Friends

- Are you close to people who are like family but not related by blood or marriage?
- Do you schedule a night out or in with friends on a regular basis?
- Do you consult with one or more people about big changes you wish to make?
- Do you follow the advice of anyone in particular?
- Whom do you trust with your children when you are away?

Money

- Which matters more to you: having enough money to pay the bills or having extra cash?
- Are you living paycheck-to-paycheck?
- How much money do you save from each paycheck?
- Do you have retirement savings?
- How much debt do you have?

Community

- Is attending city council meetings a priority?
- Do you pick up trash when you are out walking the dog?
- Do you check a community calendar when you are looking for a garage sale, trying to find something to do on a weeknight, or otherwise?
- Do you belong to a specific religious tradition to which you give your time and talents?
- When was the last time you chatted with a neighbor?
- Are you a member of any nonprofit boards?
- Do you volunteer for a school or charity?

The practical decisions to make about your estate, such as who will get what, can gradually become clear as you sort out what is a feeling, what is important, and who is in your life. Instead of caring about whether the size of your estate will confirm your father's prediction that you would always be a screw-up, you can recognize he is important to your family and you want to do whatever you can to help care for him before and after you die.

Separating facts from feelings will make it possible to see the opportunities and benefits that planning has to offer.

• *Did You Know?* •

You might have taken some kind of personality assessment test. In high school, they were designed to direct clueless teenagers toward a specific career path. Magazines claim to be able to identify your ideal mate from a 10-question survey that identifies your personality based on the Myers-Briggs typology.

When assessments for the workplace gained popularity in the 1980s, your human resources department might have rolled out a company-wide assessment program to help managers better understand and communicate with employees on a daily basis or to help them work through disputes. Lumped into one of four groups associated with a flavor of ice cream, the results seemed more gimmicky than informative and helpful.

Over time, research and development have refined and specialized these assessments so the results provide surprisingly accurate, functional information about individual values and interests. If you are struggling with shifting priorities or feeling confused about how to deal with changes in your life, this is one tool that can offer some insight and direction.

Put This to Use

If you have trouble preparing a values list or putting into words what you feel is most important in your life, taking an assessment might help.

Choosing an assessment tool can be difficult when you do not know where to look. The most reputable companies work with certified professionals, including social workers, psychologists, and coaches, trained to select the best assessment to provide the kind of information you need. The specialist will then talk through the results with you, ask questions, and offer suggestions about how to use the results.

TTI Success Insights® is an assessment company that offers an assessment called Personal Interests, Attitudes and Values ™. These assessments are not free, but the information they provide can be valuable.

What This Work Can Do

Change is difficult for most people on a good day, but under the influence of grief, it can be impossible to accomplish the most mundane tasks of cooking meals and taking out the garbage. At some point in the future, your family and close friends are going to be in that same position when dealing with your death.

Maybe your family will prefer to wear red, yellow, and bright orange to the memorial service. They might even make a family trip out of scattering your ashes on the Pacific Ocean. Regardless of how your family chooses to cope with your death, you can take steps to allow them the freedom to do what they need to.

You can plan and pay for your funeral ahead of time. You might be able to arrange to polish off the mortgage, make sure your mother's assisted living bills are paid so she can spend her retirement money on cruises, add a new wing to the church, or set up a foundation to make sure your community council has an endowment for improving living conditions.

Estate planning can also help you now. By clarifying your priorities, you can plan and save in ways that will allow you to realize your goals during your lifetime and after you die. Estate planning can:

- Integrate and organize all your personal, professional, financial, and estate goals
- Preserve your assets for use now and in the future
- Provide for your family and any chosen charities
- Ensure the efficient distribution of your estate the way you want it distributed
- Save money for your estate's obligations, for example taxes, legal fees, and court costs

What Exactly is Involved

Each estate plan is different. Just no two people are identical, no plan fits all estates. Plan components are similar, and numerous books have been written about every possible aspect of estate planning.

Depending on where you live, laws could affect what you can do with your property and when you can do it. This book is geared toward California residents and the laws that come into play for those residents.

The chapters that follow will cover the basic process and some of the more detailed information about the elements of an estate plan to help you make your own. This, like any other book or template, is a resource for gathering information and generating ideas. To adopt a canned plan that is sold as cheap and easy is to get what you pay for — a bad fit and not the outcome you hope to achieve.

The goal of this book is to help you do your homework and familiarize you with terminology you need to ask questions of and have discussions with your estate-planning professionals. If you want to do the job right, find people you can trust with your hopes and dreams.

This book is not a substitute for legal advice. It provides general information to help you plan how you want to arrange your personal estate for yourself and posterity. Laws change, and how they are applied depends on a person's specific circumstances and place of residence. Do not rely on any statement in this book as specific legal advice.

CASE STUDY: HIRING AN ESTATE-PLANNING COACH

Patricia Beaugard, Executive Coach & Trainer
pat@patbeaugard.com
www.patbeaugard.com

Patricia Beaugard has experience in the field of personal and professional coaching, in addition to being a trained ITT assessment specialist. She shares some of her thoughts on how a coach can be an important part of your estate-planning team.

Facing death

Many people have a difficult time facing the idea of their own deaths, so they avoid things, like estate planning, that will remind them. Shifting the focus onto the people left behind can help. Ask what you can do to help your loved ones get through that difficult time in their lives.

It can be helpful to look at what is bothering you. What is holding you back? What are your fears? The answers could indicate some underlying concerns; they might be related to dying, to money, or to your family members. How much you will delve into these topics is based on individual preferences.

Making notes about your feelings and the thoughts that come up when you think about estate planning can be part of the process of identifying what you have and how and to whom your possessions will be distributed. And it needs to be a process: Make some notes, then set them aside for a few days or weeks. Go back to them after you have had time to think but before you ask yourself if you are clear on what you really want.

Money, stuff, and meaning

Money represents something of value because of what it can be used for. It is a form of energy. Many people work hard for their money and are attached to it. They might struggle with the idea of giving it away to others because it represents their work and accomplishments. Those who see money as energy can flow it to others because they can always get more.

People make decisions based on their emotions and their feelings. Sometimes they are not even aware of the feelings they have, so it can be helpful for another person to help them sort out those feelings. After you share your thoughts and feelings about a specific problem, such as not wanting to distribute your estate, another person can share his or her impressions of your concerns. In that way, talking can help you explore how you feel and observe the influence those feelings have on your decision, or lack thereof.

Some people get passionate. That is when making time and space to step away and thoughtfully consider feelings and decisions is helpful; you can better determine whether that passion is a serious priority or something brought on by the estate-planning process. Consider:

- Where did this passion come from?
- Has this passion been a lasting influence?
- How have you lived this passion in your life?

I have a friend in Seattle who has never had children, but she has always had dogs, and all of them are rescued animals. For her vacation, she spent time with an organization in Utah that rescues animals. She spent a week volunteering there, and she supports them financially. This is truly a value of hers because she supports it in word and deed.

Motivators and values

By looking more deeply at what matters to you — your values — you will find what drives or motivates you to choose the profession you are in, the place you live in, or the kind of volunteer work you do at which organizations.

Another way to approach this is considering who and what is important in your life: extended family, close friends, faith or spirituality, hobbies, items you collect, or the traveling you do.

If you had difficulty talking about or identifying these details, written assessments could help you determine your values in a concrete way. Do you care about making a difference in society? Not everyone does, but some people are driven by that. Are you focused on making sure your family has financial resources available to them, or do you value independence and want to foster that in your family? Maybe you see leaving your estate to your family as spoiling them.

What matters to you now might change in a few years. Look at the people or things you could never do without several years ago, and compare that to your life now. Revisiting your motivators and values on a regular basis is important, and a coach can do more than remind you to take that second, third, and fourth look. She can ask you the questions you might forget to ask yourself so your review is thorough.

Finding a coach

A life coach helps you look at and consider these complicated, difficult topics in a constructive manner. When choosing a coach, you want to decide which criteria are important to you. Do you want to work with a coach others have recommended? Do you want your coach to be certified? Do you want someone who has graduated from a coach training program? Which kind of background or experience is important to you?

CHAPTER 2
Estate-Planning Basics

According to a recent surveys by Harris Interactive :

- 64 percent of adult Americans do not have a will.

- 80 percent of Americans aged 35-44 do not have a will.

- 51 percent of married Americans with children do not have a will.

- 71 percent of adults do not have a living will.

- 49 percent of adults do not have a power of attorney for health care purposes.

- 10 percent of adults who have not prepared any part of an estate plan say it is because they do not wish to think about dying or becoming incapacitated.

- 9 percent of adults say they do not have an estate plan because they do not know who to talk to about creating one.

- 19 percent of adults say they have not created an estate plan because they lack the sufficient assets to require one.

The primary fact that these numbers reveal is most people do not plan for their deaths or what happens to their money and possessions once they are no longer around to call the shots. Many people view estate planning either as complicated, frightening, or only for the rich.

However, estate planning is neither mysterious nor incomprehensible. It is not a privilege reserved for the wealthy. Everyone can have a will. Everyone can plan for the future.

Even though estate planning does encompass a broad array of potentially complicated issues, such as federal tax law and legal language courts require, you do not need to become an expert in all these areas to have a valid will and an estate plan. All of this rests on a simple foundation: When you die, your property stays here, and so do the people you love. You have a right to speak about what happens with these things.

You can plan to be buried with your credit card or favorite jewelry, and you might even be able to arrange to be buried in your car, but the taxes and balance due on debts or liabilities must be paid, and the rest of your property must go somewhere. Your spouse and children, if you have them, might have legal claims, and all of these considerations are part of your estate.

Suppose you want your son to have your house, and you give him the keys. Your son cannot claim to own the family house just because he received the keys before you died. If you did not transfer the title to his name by executing the necessary legal documents with the required legal formalities, the house legally would still be yours. If you have not named him as beneficiary in your will, and you have other heirs or creditors who claim the house for payment, your son would not likely get it.

Without doing the necessary legal paperwork, your belongings, debts and assets, are still your belongings. If you die without a will, the state will dispose of all of it according to law because you are no longer around to do it yourself.

Beyond the material items, unexpected and potentially more complicated issues could occur leading up to your death. A heart attack or car accident could result in a coma. Who will make the decision about your medical care and the use of extraordinary means to extend your life?

The best way to ensure your wishes are carried out is to make them known in such a way that there is no doubt about what they are. This means learning the facts about what you can and cannot do and the way to ensure what you can do will be followed.

Debunking Myths

People will do, say, and believe just about anything to avoid doing things they do not want to do; estate planning is no exception. Perhaps this is where so many myths about death and taxes came from.

- **Myth: The estate tax — the "death tax" — was repealed, so there are no taxes to avoid anymore.** The federal estate tax law was repealed for one year at the beginning of 2010, according to the 2001 Economic Growth and Tax Relief Reconciliation Act. If you died during 2010, your estate did not have to pay federal estate taxes, but it was still be subject to any estate taxes that California imposed. The estate tax came back in 2011, according to the same law.

- **Myth: All I need is a will — it will take care of all of my assets.** Debts do not go away; even if a will sets aside money to pay those debts, it might not be sufficient. In that case, the assets in your estate, for example your grandchild's college fund, will be tapped to pay creditors. Additionally, a will only addresses property that is in your name only. Property that is owned jointly with survivorship rights or pay-on-death (POD) beneficiaries, such as real estate, retirement accounts, or life insurance policies, will pass to the surviving owner or go to a beneficiary. *Chapter 5 goes into more detail about wills in general, and Chapter 11 speaks specifically to California wills.*

- **Myth: Trusts are for wealthy people.** Anyone who has an asset or assets to make the subject, or res, of a trust can make a trust. A trust can eliminate or dramatically reduce the amount of estate taxes your survivors or your estate will pay if the trust is set up properly during your lifetime. Choosing the right kind of trust to suit your needs and carefully adhering to legal language will make a trust a viable option for anyone. *Chapter 6 further addresses trusts.*

- **Myth: Life insurance is not subject to estate tax, so I do not need to do any other planning.** Life insurance proceeds frequently are not subject to income tax if they are paid to someone else, such as a spouse, parents, or a charitable institution. But if you own a life insurance policy and you have not named a beneficiary, the proceeds of that policy become part of the taxable estate and your estate might be subject to state and federal estate taxes. Any person who receives the insurance proceeds will not incur income tax liability unless he or she is in a state that subjects proceeds to inheritance tax. Also, a beneficiary who owns the policy and has paid the premiums can be taxed on the proceeds minus the amount of the premiums paid. *Chapter 7 elaborates on insurance.*

- **Myth: If I do not name a beneficiary for my 401(k), my spouse still gets the money.** Assets that do not have a named beneficiary in a will or some other legal document will end up in probate court as part of your estate. This might benefit your spouse. If you want your spouse or some other person to receive the unused portion of any retirement savings accounts, he or she must be named as a beneficiary. Naming a second, or backup, beneficiary will also keep the account out of probate if the primary beneficiary is already deceased or declines the gift for some reason. *Including your retirement accounts in your estate plan is covered in Chapter 8.*

- **Myth: If I die without a will, my spouse gets everything.** In some states, this is true; in others, it is not. The laws of the state in which you live will determine who gets what, and creditors tend to be paid first. If you own property in two or more states, such as a condo in Florida, a house in California, and a cottage in Michigan, the laws of each state will be applied to the distribution of your assets. *Probate proceedings' impact on your estate are discussed in Chapter 11.*

Misinformation and partial truths about wills, trusts, and estates are widespread. People tend to listen to other people's experience, but no two estates are exactly alike, and laws differ among the states. Further, laws change. As estate tax laws change to close loopholes or take advantage of new revenue opportunities, the areas you think you already know about estate planning can become obsolete. Over time, most people buy and sell possessions such as houses, stock portfolios, antiques, and vehicles, and those changes are called changelings. Whether your estate is growing or diminishing, you need to know what you have and how you want it to be handled after your death.

Your Estate

Yes, you have one, and defining it will most likely be the most straightforward part of this entire process. Your estate is made up of everything you own, or your entire financial worth. The formula for figuring out your net worth, your true financial value, is theoretically simple:

Assets – Liabilities = Net worth

Asset: Anything a person owns or is owed. This can be money, real estate, investments, or any other tangible property.

Liability: A debt or an obligation to pay money to another person or institution. This is also called a negative balance.

Following are some examples of common assets and liabilities constituting an estate:

Assets

- Annuities
- Cars
- Cash
- Certificates of deposit
- Insurance
- Investments
- Personal property (jewelry, stamp collection, or household items, for example)
- Real estate
- Rental income
- Retirement funds
- Savings and checking accounts
- Stock certificates
- Structured settlements (lottery winnings or lawsuit settlements, for example)

Liabilities

Bills/debts:
- Alimony
- Automobile payments
- Child support
- Credit card balances
- Future debt (a child's college tuition or parents' care, for example)
- Student loans
- Insurance premiums
- Mortgages (first- and second-home equities)
- Personal loans
- Taxes

Because it is important to keep your list of assets updated, you might consider using a digital camera to make a visual inventory of your assets so you can create an archive of these items. When documenting a dollar value for each, such as the appraisal of a necklace, you can scan that appraisal and make it part of the electronic archive. You can also collect and scan any other documents, such as stock certificates, purchase invoices, or a house deed.

These documents will be essential when meeting with estate-planning advisors, so collecting them in a secure, fireproof safe as you build your inventory will save time later.

People

You never know how many friends you have until you win the lottery; the same can be true about your death. Some people never know how many creditors, lost family, and illegitimate children they have until their will is made part of the public record. After you are legally declared dead, your will must be entered with the probate court, and it then becomes public record. Anyone who wants to make a claim against your estate can do so, and that is when the real work begins for those who helped you with your planning.

To make sure your wishes are understood and carried out, you need to make sure the people connected with your estate planning do as you choose, not what is most convenient for them.

Paid professional planners; those who carry out your wishes, such as executors, secondary executors, or legal guardians; and others such as the court, creditors, and beneficiaries will have a say in what happens after you are gone. Some people are outside your control, such as the court judge and unforeseen claimants, but you can choose those who will serve as the representatives who manage your estate.

Estate-planning professionals

Yes, there are people who actually enjoy estate-planning work. What might seem like torture to you is a challenging, rewarding career for someone who likes helping people sort out and plan for the future. The fees they charge can be an hourly rate, a per-document fee, or an ongoing estate-management fee. Be sure you understand what the charges are and how they are paid. If there is a contract, read the fine print.

Lawyer

Also called attorneys, lawyers can specialize in specific aspects of estate planning, such as wills, trusts, or probate procedure, or they might have a broader focus, such as estate planning or tax law. Depending on the size of your estate, you might need to consult with more than one lawyer to make sure you properly prepare for all the legal issues related to your estate. Some law firms have multiple members who can do all your work in-house under the direction of your lead lawyer. Or, you might feel more comfortable having different firms work on different parts of your estate plan. No matter how you approach this, you need to be forthcoming about all your personal goals and estate-planning wishes with everyone involved so they support, not undermine or contradict, each other.

Certified public accountant (CPA)

Accountants can specialize in various aspects of financial estate matters such as trusts, annuities, and estate tax law, but they also serve as estate-planning specialists who can help you consider all financial decisions. An accountant must be current on tax law and other legal requirements related to accounting for money. Like a law firm, an accounting firm might have several people on staff who specialize in different areas. But the same caution applies: Be comfortable with your CPA, because he or she has to be trusted with all the same personal information to be able to work well with the others on your team.

Financial planner

All kinds of financial planners are out there, such as Certified Financial Planner® (CFP®) and Chartered Financial Analyst (CFA). But all of them analyze a person's overall financial situation and, in conjunction with their client, develop a comprehensive plan to meet his or her financial goals and objectives. Certified planners have followed a specific course of education or taken training classes, and some go on to develop expertise in specific areas, such as estate or retirement planning. Financial planners can help you prepare your estate to achieve a target value by a certain age or for a projected time of death. Be wary of anyone who is self-taught or who works on 100 percent commission. The advice you get might not necessarily be based on the most current information or be in your best interest. Commissioned sales people have an interest in selling specific products to earn their livelihood, which might not coincide with your needs or your pocketbook.

Insurance agent

Gone are the days when an insurance sales person appeared at your door and offered to spend hours chatting with you about your insurance needs, including home, auto, and life. Today, representatives go through human resources departments to coordinate long-term and short-term disability coverage for company employees, which employers might partially pay for. Medical and dental insurance, not to mention pet insurance, long-term care insurance, and other less common insurance plans, are now sold over the phone or on the Internet. An actual insurance agent can help you with your estate planning by assessing the type and amount of insurance you need and can afford. A real agent, rather than call center staff, is the better person to speak to about your insurance needs, and if you cannot find one, your other estate-planning professionals might be able to help.

Coaches

Financial, professional, and personal coaches can help you identify and manage monetary, career, and personal goals. At a time when mixed messages about being loyal to your employer and diversifying your stock portfolio make you wonder what you should do about the stock options your company offers, a coach can help you sort out the implications of selling or keeping those options and the potential impact on your career and estate plan. A coach's goal is to see you succeed, not make sure a corporation thrives or your beneficiaries get a chunk of change. A coach is an objective third party who is also hired to focus primarily on what is best for you. Training and a comfortable level of communication are critical to in a coach who will be a good fit for your needs. There are certification courses for various forms of coaching, but there are no national standards, and formal training is not required for coaches. This means you must ask specific questions about the person's experience, training, and references.

Spiritual advisor

The altruistic efforts of many people are based on their chosen faith traditions or their own moral compasses. Some difficult decisions about personal matters are not related to accounting or legal issues. For example, you might be trying to decide whether your drug-addicted brother will be helped or hurt by a large inheritance as part of your estate planning. Choosing charitable institutions to benefit from your life's work might be another consideration. Changes in your life, such as divorce or the unexpected death of a loved one, might necessitate changes in your will at a time when the family member you would normally discuss those things with is grieving. A minister, priest, rabbi, or other faith consultant can offer guidance, support, and information in line with your belief system that might be helpful in these situations. Someone to talk to about personal matters related to family decisions especially speaks to the values and priorities you identified early in your estate-planning process.

Whether you need any or all of these people in their various roles to participate in planning your estate is up to the types of issues that bother you about the process. Though some do not charge anything, others might have flat rates or hourly charges. The money you invest, much like the time you invest, is valuable, so be sure you weigh the short-term costs against the long-term gains.

If you choose to use more than one person to help you plan, consider choosing one person to serve as the primary contact through which all information will flow. If you choose a lawyer to serve as your point person, which is usually the best choice, he or she would work with the other professionals on your team to collect information and clarify their part of your estate management. Then, he or she would meet with you and go through the information. A time-saving efficiency for you, this will cost a little extra because you need to pay your lawyer to do this coordination work, but in the long run, you will have a reliable, well-informed person who can serve in your stead when you are gone and who understands the complete picture of your estate and your intentions.

☑ Choosing an Estate Planner

Estate Planner Qualities and Characteristics

Qualifications for estate-planning professionals will vary based on their professional focus and expertise. Individual training is important, but there are some fundamental skills that all of them should have. Scrutinize prospective estate-planning team members before and after you meet with them. They will be privy to your most personal and private information.

Before: Do some homework before you meet with a planner.

☐ Is your estate planner ethical? Check with the Better Business Bureau and any related professional organizations, such as the American Bar Association for lawyers, to find out whether any complaints have been filed or reprimand proceedings have taken place.

☐ How well does your planner interact with clients? Get references from current clients to find out about the positives and negatives of working with this person. Some questions to ask his or her current clients could include:

   o   Is this person prepared for meetings, and does he or she follow through on tasks that need to be done afterward?

   o   How well does this person collaborate with other estate-planning professionals?

   o   Do you spend much time in the waiting area before an appointment?

   o   Have you ever had mistakes on your invoices?

   o   Have your meetings ever been canceled on short notice?

☐ Which professional associations is your planner a part of? If this person is the member of an organization, call and ask about his or her involvement and for referrals.

☐ Which services does your planner offer? Find out the range of services this person offers, or whether he or she works in collaboration with others inside or outside his or her company.

☐ Is your planner considerate? Willingness to listen to your concerns and needs is essential; review his or her website and any promotional materials for signs of this trait.

After: When you meet with an estate-planning professional for the first time, pay attention to the level of comfort or discomfort you feel, and evaluate that meeting soon afterward. These are a few questions to ask:

☐ Did he or she ask you relevant questions?

☐ Which did he or she do more: talk or listen?

☐ Did he or she tell you what you should do or present you with options to consider?

☐ Did this person disclose any commissions or other benefits he or she receives from the institutions offering the products he or she represents? For example, out of three different kinds of insurance you talked about, he or she might receive a commission for one.

☐ Did he or she explain things in a way that you could understand?

☐ Was he or she willing to go back over details until you were clear about confusing points?

☐ Were you given fees and hourly rates in writing?

☐ Are you expected to sign a contract?

☐ Were you given a timeline or some other expectation for how long this process might take?

☐ Did you feel you were being helped or seen as nothing more than a revenue stream?

CASE STUDY: WHAT IT TAKES TO BE A FINANCIAL ADVISOR

U.S. Department of Labor
Bureau of Labor Statistics
www.dol.gov

Estate planning is a specialty within the field of financial planning, and the U.S. Department of Labor's Bureau of Labor Statistics predicts this is going to be a growing industry for many years.

Beyond that, the bureau also provides job descriptions and other information about various industries, including financial advisors and planners. This material provides a description of the kind of work a planner might do in a day and the characteristics of a person who is successful in this kind of position. You might not be looking to make a career change, but this can serve as excellent background material when you begin looking for an estate planner to help you develop your plan.

Financial analysts and personal financial advisors

Significant points:

- Good interpersonal skills and an aptitude for working with numbers are among the most important qualifications for financial analysts and personal financial advisors.
- Those who have earned a professional designation or an MBA are expected to have the best opportunity to succeed in these highly paid positions. Competition is expected to be high despite rapid job growth.
- Almost one-third of personal financial advisors are self-employed.

Nature of the work:

Financial analysts and personal financial advisors provide analysis and guidance to businesses and individuals making investment decisions. Both types of specialists gather financial information, analyze it, and make recommendations. However, their job duties differ because of the type of investment information they provide and their relationships with investors.

Personal financial advisors assess the financial needs of individuals. Advisors use their knowledge of investments, tax laws, and insurance to recommend financial options to individuals. They help them to identify and plan to meet short- and long-term goals. Planners help clients with retirement and estate planning, funding the college education of children, and other general investment choices. Many also provide tax advice or sell life insurance. Although most planners offer advice on a wide range of topics, some specialize in areas, such as retirement and estate planning or risk management.

Personal financial advisors tend to work with many clients, and they often must find their own customers. Many personal financial advisors spend a large portion of their time making sales calls and marketing their services. Many advisors also meet potential clients by giving seminars or lectures or using business and social contacts. Finding clients and building a customer base is one of the most important aspects of becoming successful as a financial advisor.

Financial advisors begin work with a client by setting up a consultation. This is often a face-to-face meeting in which the advisor obtains as much information as possible about the client's finances and goals. The advisor then develops a comprehensive financial plan that identifies problem areas; recommends improvement; and selects appropriate investments compatible with the client's goals, attitude toward risk, and expectation or need for a return on the investment.

Sometimes this plan is written, but more often it is in the form of verbal advice. Advisors sometimes meet with accountants or legal professionals for help.

Financial advisors tend to meet with established clients at least once a year to update them on potential investments and adjust their financial plan for any life changes, such as marriage, disability, or retirement. Financial advisors also answer clients' questions about changes in benefit plans or changes in their jobs or careers. Financial planners must educate their clients about risks so the clients do not have unrealistic expectations.

Most personal financial advisors buy and sell financial products, such as securities and life insurance. Fees and commissions from the purchase and sale of securities and life insurance plans are one of the major sources of income for most personal financial advisors.

Education and training:

A bachelor's or master's degree is required for financial analysts and is strongly preferred for personal financial advisors.

Employers usually do not require a specific field of study for personal financial advisors, but a bachelor's degree in accounting, finance, economics, business, mathematics, or law provides good preparation for the occupation. Courses in investments, taxes, estate planning, and risk management are also helpful. Programs in financial planning are becoming more widely available in colleges and universities.

Licensure:

Almost all personal financial advisors need the Series 7 and Series 63 or 66 licenses. These licenses give their holders the right to act as a registered representative of a securities firm and to give financial advice. Because the Series 7 license requires sponsorship, self-employed personal financial advisors must maintain a relationship with a large securities firm. This relationship allows them to act as representatives of that firm in the buying and selling of securities.

If personal financial advisors choose to sell insurance, they need additional licenses state licensing boards issue.

Other qualifications:

Strong math, analytical, and problem-solving skills are essential qualifications for financial analysts. Good communication skills also are necessary, because these workers must present complex financial concepts and strategies. Self-confidence, maturity, and the ability to work independently are important as well. Financial analysts must be detail-oriented, motivated to seek out obscure information, and familiar with the workings of the economy, tax laws, and money markets. Financial analysts should also be comfortable with computers. Although most of the software they use is proprietary, they must be comfortable working with spreadsheets and statistical packages.

Personal financial advisors need many of the same skills, but they must emphasize customer service. They need strong sales skills, including the ability to make customers feel comfortable. It is important for them to be able to present financial concepts to clients with language that is easy to understand. Personal financial advisors must also be able to interact casually with people from many different backgrounds. Some advisors have experience in a related occupation, such as accountancy, auditing, selling insurance, or brokering.

Who Will Carry Out Your Wishes in Your Place?

At the heart of estate planning is the recognition that at some point in time, you are going to die, and before then, you might become incompetent. When that happens, someone else has to take responsibility for your estate. This responsibility will involve both people and property.

Determining who will serve as the legal guardian of minor children is a huge decision and a tremendous responsibility for whomever agrees to be responsible for the health and well-being of your children. A guardian of a minor — any adult legally appointed to be responsible for the needs of your children until they reach legal age — is not the same as a guardian for an adult. The guardian of an adult is legally appointed to manage the affairs of an incompetent or infirm adult of any age. A mentally challenged 32-year-old brother could need a guardian as much as a parent in the early stages of Alzheimer's disease.

Equally important is the executor of your estate. An executor, also called a personal representative, is the individual who handles the property you are leaving behind. If you die without a will, the court appoints an administrator, frequently a spouse or adult child. This person's fiduciary obligation is to make sure your assets and liabilities are disposed of in a legal, efficient, and thoughtful manner. The money necessary to support your children, a disabled sibling, or your aging parents will be in the hands of your executor.

Legal guardians

Appointing the guardianship of another person, whether for a child or an adult, is legal action. The court appoints a guardian based on the wishes of the person making the request. A child's godparents do not automatically become guardians upon your death; you have to put guardianship in writing in a will. If you are the legal guardian of your elderly mother, you need to make provisions for her care in your will in the event that you die before she does.

The guardian for a minor will be responsible for food, clothing, and shelter. However, he or she also will be responsible for managing assets in the child's name and providing education and health care. The same can be true for an adult's guardian, who might also be responsible for paying bills and making sure the home is cleaned on a regular basis.

Choosing any guardian is difficult because of the responsibilities involved. The most obvious concern is selecting someone who will care for your family the way you would, but more important is whether the person will follow through on the commitment. A person in her 20s in the midst of building a career might say she is willing to set aside her career to care for her sister's young children. But after three years, will she still be willing to stay at home with the children even if money is not an issue?

Consider some of the following characteristics:

- **Age:** Being young or old is as much about experience as age. Do you want the person taking care of your children to be your same age?

- **Lifestyle:** Your sister is not religious, but you want your children to attend a Catholic church. Will she take them to church every Sunday?

- **Skills in caring for children or adults:** Patience and the knowledge of where to find and seek help as needed are essential. Is the person you are considering good with children?

- **Marital status:** Your divorced brother is fabulous with your boys, but would two parents be better for your children? Would your sister and her husband be better?

- **Compatibility:** If your children hate your sister's husband, this is not going to be a good long-term fit. How do your children act around the person you are considering?

- **Money skills:** Your aunt is a penny pincher, but your uncle is a spendthrift. How would they handle the money set aside for your brother's group home bills?

You also need to consider your expectations for your children and how many of those you want to impose on the people who will become their new parents. Once you come up with the priorities you have for your children, make a list of several people. Ask each of them whether they would be willing to serve as guardians under the conditions that you lay out. It is a bad idea to name someone as guardian without his or her knowledge. If that person refuses, the court will then decide what is in the best interest of the minors or others in need of care. You might not like the people the court chooses.

A secondary or backup guardian will address the gap left by people who might be unable to serve in that capacity.

• *Did You Know?* •

A property guardian or property manager is a legal adult who takes responsibility for the oversight of property a minor inherited. Children under the age of 18 can inherit property, but they are only allowed to legally own that property with adult supervision; an adult must have the responsibility of managing it. Just because a 17-year-old can inherit a car does not mean he or she is in charge of it.

Becoming the legal guardians of children might be enough responsibility for the people you select to provide for their upbringing. If the burden of managing their property on top of that is too much, another person can be appointed for that role.

Put This to Use

Harry and Sally set up an education trust for their three minor children, Huey, Dewy, and Louis, in addition to putting the house and all other assets in their names. They are enrolled in private schools and will continue to live in their home; Aunt Blanche will move in with them.

Blanche has a good heart but is so bad with money she forgets to make her own house payment. Putting her in charge of paying tuition from the proper accounts and the property taxes on time is a disaster waiting to happen. So, Harry and Sally named their long-time banker and trust officer, Bill Smith, as the property manager. He also knows Blanche, so she can easily call him to ask for help if he needs to pay additional school fees.

This frees her to focus on the boys instead of on the finances.

An added bonus is Bill, as a trust officer for a bank, is not likely to get away with embezzling money from the trusts. Bill cannot be paid a fee, which means more money for the trust.

☑ Choosing a Guardian

You, your children, a sibling, or a parent might one day need another person to make decisions that you, or they — would normally make. Asking someone else to take on your responsibilities in addition to their own is a significant request that carries legal, ethical, and moral implications. Here are details to consider when making a list of people you might want to ask to serve in this capacity:

☐ **Eligibility:** Different states have different rules about this. If you move, be sure to check whether your named guardians are still allowed to serve.

☐ **Common ideals:** People who have similar views about child rearing and hold similar values and religious beliefs are more likely to raise your children or care for your adult family members in the way that you would.

☐ **Compassion:** They might need to address the emotional and practical issues and needs that come up as a result of your death.

☐ **Flexibility:** Different people react differently to dramatic changes in life, so it might be necessary for the guardian to take time off work or move to a new home to address the needs of his or her charge.

☐ **Emotional stability:** Grief is a reasonable response to death, but a person who is prone to depression or has mental health issues might not be able to care for others during such a critical time.

☐ **Marital status:** Some people prefer children have a two-parent family; others are more focused on the personality of the guardian. Being single might mean more flexibility. Consider what is most important to you, and be true to that criterion.

☐ **Location:** If the guardian is unable to move into your home or be close to whom he or she needs to take care of, those children or adults might have to move. This could create additional stresses for them.

Things to keep in mind

- Some family members might not be happy with your choice of guardian or believe you made the best choice. Be prepared to address fears, concerns, frustrations, and even anger with those who disagree with your choices.

- Always discuss the expectations and responsibilities with the potential guardian before naming that person in a will or other legal document.

- If it makes you both feel more comfortable, spell out your expectations for each guardian in writing so you are both clear about your wishes.

- Always choose secondary and tertiary guardians in the event that unexpected situations, such as the death of your first choice before your own, or life circumstances, such as serious illness or a job transfer to another country, make it impossible for that person to agree to be a guardian.

- Be aware the court might decide your choices for a guardian are not suitable. For example, if your brother was recently arrested on drunk driving charges, a judge might choose another guardian based on what he or she thinks is in the best interest of the child or person in need of a guardian. This is when naming secondary and tertiary guardians can help guide the court.

Executor

Just as you need to carefully select your guardians, you need to consider who will manage the affairs of your estate. *See Chapter 5 for more information on the responsibilities of an executor.*

The following list offers a quick summary of his or her duties:

- Making sure your will is accepted as valid in the probate process This also means defending the will against any challenges.

- Collecting your assets.

- Overseeing the transition of gifts made to beneficiaries. This might include a title transfer for a house or a life insurance policy check made out to the correct person.

- Reviewing, evaluating, and paying any claims against your estate. These commonly include taxes and outstanding bills.

- Raising the money to pay claims. This could mean selling assets, such as a house or car.

- Preparing and filing an account of all financial transactions for the court.

The person who takes on this task must know what is involved. For this reason, choosing a secondary executor is a good idea; if you do not appoint one, the court will appoint one for your estate.

Choosing an Executor or Trustee

Choosing an executor or a trustee is highly personal, so no definition or approach will work for everyone. Some details to consider are:

☐ **Integrity:** Can you trust this person in any circumstance?

☐ **Your relationship:** Does this person know you well enough personally and professionally to know how you might want things handled?

☐ **Personality:** How will this person deal with a grieving family when decisions must be made?

☐ **Thoughtfulness:** Will this person consider questions and demands creditors, beneficiaries, the court, or anyone contesting your will and wishes make on your estate?

☐ **Common sense:** When given multiple choices, does this person tend to be practical?

☐ **Realism:** If this person does not know what to do, will he or she seek the advice of experts?

☐ **Potential conflicts of interest:** Could decisions made by this person benefit others, including your trustee or executor, and harm your family?

☐ **Asset management skills:** What experience does this person have with real estate and financial markets, for example?

☐ **Real-estate management skills:** Is this person informed about what it takes to maintain and manage property, whether a house or undeveloped piece of land, in your estate?

☐ **Knowledge of beneficiaries:** Can this person accurately assess the needs of your beneficiaries without your daily guidance?

☐ **Criminal background:** Has this person ever been convicted of a crime related to the responsibilities you are asking of him or her?

Additional considerations and notes:

_____

_____

_____

People of Influence

After you are gone, the legal pecking order of the people who will have the most influence over what happens to your estate are the probate court, creditors, and your beneficiaries.

Probate court judge

Specifics about how probate court accepts, records, and addresses issues with wills are addressed in Chapter 11.

Probate court is part of a state's court system. Some states have special judges who only handle estate settlement cases whereas others might not specialize in that way. In California, superior trial courts of general jurisdiction handle probate. Regardless of the laws governing the organizational structure of the court, a probate judge will review the legal documents related to an estate. If a person dies without a will, the judge will appoint an administrator who serves in the same capacity as an executor. He or she also will ask for and review details such as the will, if there is one; the inventory of assets; and petitions from creditors and heirs. Heir is the legal title of a person who inherits property from an estate that does not have a will, or is intestate. Beneficiaries are those who receive an inheritance by being named in a legal document such as a will or trust.

The judge will supervise the process of settling your estate and will only adjudicate, or hand down decisions, as they are needed, such as when a creditor makes a claim and the administrator denies payment. The same could happen when a person comes forward and claims to be an heir to your estate.

The judge might choose someone you think is unsuitable for the job of administrator, and he or she might agree to pay the claim of an old business partner you do not feel you owe. You can prevent these situations from happening by creating an estate plan and avoiding probate when possible.

Probate judges also establish guardianship and handle other special circumstances, such as bigamy, romantic partners who want part of an estate, or children you did not know about who contest decisions about heirs.

Creditors

Your debts are paid first, so how much you owe other people at the time of your death will determine how much of your estate goes to your loved ones and charities. Some creditors might not make a claim against your estate. You might have borrowed $5,000 from Aunt Henrietta and she does not care about being paid back. When your executor writes a check, she simply tears it up and hands it back.

Outstanding credit card balances, a personal line of credit from a bank, and a car loan are a few examples of the bills you might be paying when you are alive, and these must be settled after your death. In addition to letting creditors know about your death, your executor will request the amount of payment necessary to settle your accounts. Some companies, upon reading a death notice, might try to make a claim of payments due. It is up to the executor or administrator — or the probate judge, if this becomes necessary — to determine whether a claim is legitimate and must be paid.

Beneficiaries

Even if you die intestate, which means to die without leaving a will, a number of will substitutes make it possible for your estate to avoid probate completely: joint ownership of property wherein the surviving partner automatically takes full control; revocable and irrevocable trusts; life insurance, pensions, and annuities with named beneficiaries; and stocks, bonds, and bank accounts paid to a designated person upon the death of the owner.

If a beneficiary is not named or the primary beneficiary declines the bequest or is dead and a secondary beneficiary is not named, the probate court judge will decide who receives the unclaimed property.

Beneficiaries and court-named heirs can challenge decisions you or the court made about an inheritance. People who believe they should have received an inheritance or who only received a fraction of what they were told they would get or think they deserve can challenge the will or court ruling. These challenges can hold up the resolution of your estate for months or years, so making sure your legal documents are in order can help reduce this problem.

These basic elements of an estate plan describe what is involved and who is integral to the process. Next are the components of an estate plan — the documents, accounts, and policies that make it all legal and taxable.

CASE STUDY: DETAILS AND LEGALESE DO MATTER

Scott M. Slovin, Esq.
Schwartz Manes Ruby & Slovin
sslovin@smrslaw.com
www.smrslaw.com

What are some essentials of an estate plan?

The biggest concern in an estate plan is coordinating all of the estate plan documents. These include the will, with the trust and beneficiary designations, and ownership of assets, including payable-on-death or transfer-on-death assets. Essential information includes the following:

- The name of the testator, the person preparing the will, or the grantor or settlor, the name of the person creating the trust
- Beneficiaries' names and relationships to the testator or the grantor and alternate beneficiaries in case a beneficiary predeceases the testator or grantor
- The fiduciaries, the executor or trustee, and the guardians for the minor children

- The way estate taxes and other expenses of the estate will be paid and from which assets the cash will be drawn

The benefits of working with an attorney are to avoid mistakes in drafting, such as failing to specify from which assets taxes will be paid or being unclear about bequests, and to reduce federal and state estate taxes that a lawyer who does not do estate planning or someone who is not an attorney might fail to take into consideration.

Why is it important to use legal terms in estate-planning documents? So many of them are confusing.

There is a long history of interpretation under state law and federal tax law, and attorneys like to use language that they know has been interpreted by the courts to achieve the results they are seeking for clients. Attorneys are trying to simplify their language and create wills and trusts that are easier for clients to follow.

How does a person go about choosing a professional in your field?

The best way to choose an estate-planning attorney is to seek the recommendation of financial planners, accountants, and insurance agents who work with estate-planning attorneys. Make sure you choose someone who works with more than a couple of wills per year. You need to find someone who spends at least half of his or her time in estate planning so he or she understands all of the nuances of state probate, estate law, and tax law. Especially important would be attorneys who have extra training in the field of estate planning and tax planning. Recommendations of friends and neighbors would also be important.

CHAPTER 3
Components of an Effective Estate Plan

Car keys, directions, map, water bottle, and snacks: the basics of what you need for a road trip are easy to identify and collect. The car does not go anywhere without the keys, and directions are essential for reaching the final destination. The way you plan to achieve the goals of your estate planning can be equally simple once you know what is necessary.

Those who have taken this trip before, from specialized and highly trained professionals to those who have learned from personal experience, have prepared plenty of guidebooks and maps just like those you would use to take a road trip to a new place. Those people can help you do the things that will make your trip suited to you, and you do not need to use up time and energy figuring it all out on your own. The components of an effective estate plan are all the same; the pieces that match your goals and the way those components work together is what individualizes each plan.

Although legalese is involved, you can use everyday words for the same thing. It is like when a road has a state route number, a formal name, and a name the locals gave it. Knowing the description of something is enough to gain the necessary understanding so you can still find your way when the map is confusing.

Legally Speaking

A court only recognizes legally binding documents as the way to give your estate to others. Some of these are so widely known and commonly used that descriptions and definitions don't seem necessary. Most people know what a will is and what it is for. But the difference between what makes a document legal and what you think makes a document legal can get you in trouble. If you do not have the correct wording, the correct number of witnesses, or the correct types of witnesses, all of your efforts can be ignored.

The following are reoccurring terms you will find throughout this book. Some definitions will be expanded upon in sections that provide more detailed information.

- **Property:** The things you own, which can be anything you want to give to other people; also referred to as principal.

- **Real property:** This is any kind of real estate.

  o **Types:** One type is vacant land you buy with the intention of building on or an investment you plan to sell later without developing is one type. Other types are your primary residence; a second home, such as a vacation condo; a portion of a home, such as a timeshare; investment property, such as a two-family house you own that generates rental income; or property in which you share ownership with a partner or business.

- **Personal property:** Your possessions. This category is further divided into tangible personal property, things you can touch, and intangible personal property, or financial assets.

  o **Tangible:** Jewelry; artwork; furniture; china; collectibles, such as figurines or antique books; electronic equipment; cars; and boats you have.

o **Intangible:** Checking accounts; savings accounts; money market funds; mutual funds; stocks; bonds; or retirement accounts such as a pension, an individual retirement arrangement (IRA), a Roth IRA, or a Keogh plan you have.

- **Property interest:** This refers to the connection you have to a specific item, piece of land, or other belongings.

  o **Legal interest:** Property you can legally transfer or manage but is not yours to use or keep for yourself. Someone who is responsible for the maintenance and oversight of the use of a piece of property but does not legally own it is called a trustee.

    ▶ *Example: Steve manages the house and grounds of his great-grandmother Julie's family home because she lives in a nursing home. He calls a plumber and contracts to have the backed-up drains fixed. Steve might even place an ad in the paper to rent the house, screen applicants, and serve as the primary contract for the renter by collecting rent and addressing problems. But the property is in Julie's name, and Steve cannot sell the house or any of the land because it belongs to her.*

  o **Beneficial interest:** You receive a benefit from the property.

    ▶ *Example: Veronica always wanted to go to art school, but she thought the tuition was too expensive even with student loans. After she graduated from high school, her grandfather told her he set up a trust fund for her, and the proceeds from that trust will pay her tuition and fees for art school.*

- **Ownership:** What the individual or individuals who hold the legal title to a piece of property have. The ability to retain, sell, or give away this property depends on the number of people who hold that title and, in some cases, their relationship and any legal agreements or contracts connected to the property.

o **Sole ownership:** A single person holds the title to the property.

▶ *Example: Mandy owns her car because she paid cash for it, and the title of the car is in her name.*

o **Joint ownership:** When any two people hold an equal share of the title to a piece of property. The most common form is spousal, for example when a legally married couple has both names on a title to a piece of property.

▶ *Example: Joe and Mary are listed on the mortgage and the deed to the home they live in together.*

• **Community property:** Property owned equally by a wife and husband by state law. California is a community property state, which has a particular legal significance upon estate planning for married people. Other community property states are Arizona, Idaho, Louisiana, Nevada, New Mexico, Texas, Washington, and Wisconsin.

▶ *Example: When Clyde and Bonnie divorced, everything they owned that was not a specific gift from a family member or something owned before or after the marriage was lumped together and divided into two equal parts.*

• **Separate property:** Things owned by one spouse that are not part of the couple's community property.

▶ *Example: Fred owned an antique Model A Ford before he and Carrie married, and the title is in his name.*

- **Joint tenancy:** A group of people hold equal and undivided title to a piece of property. Joint tenancy is recognized in California and community property with right of survivorship.

  ▶ *Example:* Brian, Joseph, and Greg own a cottage together in Michigan. All their names are on the deed to the property, and they schedule their vacation time so everyone has an opportunity to use the cottage.

- **Exemption:** This is a specific amount of money estate taxes will not affect. Federal and state governments often set an amount that is tax-free. Taxes would be due on any amount beyond. In 2010, no federal estate tax existed, but it was reinstatement with a threshold exemption in 2011. Estate tax was phased out in California. According to the California State Controller's Office, a "California Estate Tax Return is not required to be filed for decedents whose date of death is after December 31, 2004."

- **Donor:** The person who gives a gift or bequest.

- **Beneficiary:** The individual(s) or group(s) that will receive the property in a will or trust. This can be a single person, a group of people, one group, several groups, or a combination of any of these.

- **Distribution:** The disbursement or payment of property from an account to a beneficiary. It could be in the form of a check or another monetary payment, or it could be the transfer of a title into the name of the beneficiary.

Defining Your Estate

Understanding what property is and how ownership is determined makes it possible for you to define your estate. Making a list of what constitutes your estate and what makes up the estate of a spouse or life partner will make it easier to understand some of the choices you have for creating your own plan.

This list, combined with the fundamental values you defined in Chapter 2, will help you consider how a specific estate-planning component might be a good tool for you. Having some information about your estate in mind while you learn can make the process go more smoothly.

Pass the Parchment

Many important books and legal documents were printed on parchment. Only the wealthy could read or write or afford to buy parchment for their private use and for special occasions, such as drafting the Declaration of Independence. Even though most of the documents that make up your retirement plan will not have the same historical impact as that document had, it is important to make sure your documents are complete and accurate. If you forget a clause or use the wrong word, the directions you leave will not be worth the paper they are printed on.

What the document is, what it can do, and the laws affecting it will help you choose the elements of your estate plan that will transform your thoughts and wishes into action.

Will

What it is:

A legal document in which you identify the people or institutions that should receive money and property from your estate after your death. It also serves to appoint guardianship of children or adults who are your legal responsibility and designate an executor to manage your estate after you die.

What it does:

- It spells out your instructions and wishes for what you want done with the property you leave behind.

- Your affairs go from being private to public when you use a will because it becomes a part of public record. If you want privacy, keep your will basic and legal. *For more information on this, see Chapter 5.*

The laws that matter:

- State laws govern the execution of the instructions in a will.

- A judge can challenge a will and overturn directions contained within it.

Potential problems:

- The extremes of thinking a will is unnecessary or is all you need limits your estate plan's effectiveness.

- Using a will form from the store or the Internet. Unless you know the laws of California and how the language of that document matches up, you could have a false sense of security about what will happen after your death.

Will substitute

What it is:

An agreement, contract, or other legal arrangement that accomplishes the same goals to protect and transfer property rights but without the use of a will document. Some options are:

- Holding property in a living trust or joint tenancy.

- Owning a monetary account, such as a savings account, which is set up to automatically transfer ownership to the beneficiary upon the death of the donor. This is also known as a payable-on-death account.

- Financial arrangements that have a named beneficiary, including life insurance, IRAs, or pension plans.

What it does:

- These arrangements can save time because the ownership automatically transfers to the beneficiary upon the death of the donor, so it skips the probate process.

- Privacy is preserved, again, because the substitute does not go through probate and is not subject to open records laws.

- They can also save money because probate court fees are not needed, and some estate taxes can be avoided.

- A will substitute could address more complicated situations, such as multiple ex-spouses and blended families with children from previous marriages.

The laws that matter:

- Tax laws of California and the federal government matter. There is a significant amount of misinformation about what is tax-exempt and what is not.

Potential problems:

- Each form of will substitute has its own quirks and legal requirements, and missing details, such as not having enough signatures, witnesses, or clauses, could nullify the entire document. Using the wrong language can also submarine your efforts.

- Find a qualified professional to help you close all the holes in your documents.

Trust

What it is:

A legal arrangement that transfers property from the original owner to a person or company. The trust holds and maintains the property for the benefit of a specific individual, group of people, or institution(s).

What it does:

Depending on the kind of trust and the beneficiary, the legal arrangement will either hold any property in a tax-free account until distributions are made to people or institutions other than the donor or until the entire trust is turned over to a beneficiary.

The laws that matter:

- Tax laws matter. Some trusts are tax-exempt. The beneficiary must pay taxes on some trusts when distributions are made or the ownership of the trust changes from your name to the beneficiary. Be sure to know what the tax implications are; not all trusts are created equal.

- Exemptions also apply here. Trusts for education, a spouse, and other reasons can eliminate taxes in the distribution or transfer of a trust.

Potential problems:

- Choosing a trust that will not achieve the results you want is a problem. Many sales reps will make a commission off the trust you establish, so they might be looking at how to maximize their profit.

- Thinking a trust is all you need is another problem.

Insurance

What it is:

A method of protecting valuables in the form of a policy in which premiums are paid over time to guarantee a specific payment for a specific purpose by the company accepting the premiums. Those valuables can be property, such as a home, car, or jewelry; a person's life; or the ability to work and care for yourself, which life, disability, health care, and long-term care insurance covers.

What it does:

- These various policies protect an estate from the devastation an unexpected accident or terrible illness can bring to your finances. They can preserve your assets and allow you to spend or distribute them as you choose.

- For a small investment, insurance can dramatically increase the value of your estate.

- Some insurance policies only pay a percentage, so what you receive depends on another factor, such as your income. Long-term disability might only replace 50 percent of your pre-disability income, for example.

The laws that matter:

- Tax laws matter. Know which insurance income is taxable. Depending on the age of the beneficiary, disability insurance payments, death benefits, and other kinds of insurance might be subject to local, state, and federal income taxes or estate taxes.

Potential problems:

- Buying more insurance than you can afford is a problem. Once you stop paying premiums, the policy will no longer pay benefits.

- Believing that buying insurance is all the estate planning you need to do is also a problem.

Taxes

What they are:

Estate taxes are fees federal and state governments levy against property that is left behind after a person dies. Gift taxes are fees federal and state governments levy against property that is transferred to someone before the owner dies.

What they do:

Taxes affect the amount of money your beneficiaries receive because all bills, including taxes, get paid out before your beneficiaries see any money. Carefully investigate which taxes must be paid on the property you leave behind and who is responsible for paying.

The laws that matter:

- All kinds of loopholes were created and filled over the years, so federal and state tax codes in particular can be confusing.

- This is where a professional is essential to avoid fines, late fees, and other charges on top of the taxes already owed.

Potential problems:

- Thinking that you will not have to pay any taxes after you die is a problem. You might not be around to write the check, but that does not stop the government from sending a bill.

- A failure to leave instructions for your executor about money you set aside specifically for the purpose of paying your estate's taxes could result in the sale of assets or other mistakes in the management of your affairs.

- An executor's failure to file your final income tax and the necessary estate tax forms can have serious consequences for your executor and the bequests you want others to receive.

Retirement funds and pension

What it is:

Money saved in different kinds of accounts intended to pay for living expenses after a person is no longer employed full time. There are employer-sponsored accounts, such as a profit-sharing plan, stock bonus plan, employee stock ownership plan (ESOP), and 401(k); individual accounts, such as an IRA, Roth IRA, annuity, variable annuity, or a Keogh plan; and government benefits in the form of Social Security retirement benefits, Medicare, and disability.

What it does:

- Funds saved for retirement are supposed to make it possible for seniors to live comfortably without working, but planning and correct saving are essential to achieving that goal.

- There are no guarantees. Just because you save does not mean the money will be there. As more companies renege on retirement plans and underfund employer pension contributions, the retirement you think you will have might not be possible.

The laws that matter:

- Serious financial penalties are imposed on funds removed from retirement accounts before you reach retirement age.

- Social security benefits are taxed as income.

Potential problems:

- Believing that government benefits will be enough to live on when you retire is a problem.

- Pension plans that are not insured might not deliver the benefits promised.

In the end, your estate plan might look similar to that of your spouse, or it could be completely different. It all depends on the components you value most and how you handle financial matters. Looking over the following hypothetical estate plans to see how the things you value might impact the decisions you make.

<u>"Fly first class; your children will after you are gone."</u>
Ferdie and Lilly, married 65 years with three grown,
independent daughters

Will: They wrote separate wills at the same time that leave everything to the surviving spouse with specific bequests of heirlooms to family and sentimental tokens to friends. After both are gone, everything else goes to the church in which they were married.

Living will: It contains instructions not to use any extraordinary efforts to sustain life should they experience a loss of brain function or a disease that impairs their ability to make sound decisions.

Life insurance: They already cashed out one policy to pay for an Alaskan cruise. A second policy will pay for funeral expenses for the first one who dies, and the last policy will be used for the survivor.

Pension plan: They spend the dividends every month; whatever is left goes into the travel fund.

Living trust: They spending the dividends every month and use the rest for road trips.

Charitable trust: All property is held in trust for the church and the animal rescue and shelter.

<u>"Yours, Mine, and Mine"</u>
Andrea, divorced with no children and single
for more than 40 years

Will: Andrea does not have one. She rents a houseboat, and all her possessions fit into whatever car she leases, so she has nothing to bequest.

Living will: She does not have one.

Life insurance: Andrea has three policies — one for Mom, one for Dad, and one for all death-related expenses.

Disability insurance: Insurance policies she has include short-term, long-term, and extended-care.

Retirement accounts: Her 401(k), Roth IRA, and stock bonus plans will cover her monthly expenses, and whatever is left goes into a rainy day account.

Trust: This document covers her cabin and land she owns on Whidbey Island in Washington, where she plans to retire.

<u>"The one with the most toys wins!"</u>
John Richard Greenman, XIV, and Maya E. Primwater,
not married and do not have children but have lived together for 18 years

John Richard Greenman, XIV

Will: 50 percent of everything not in the trust goes to Maya; there is just enough information in the will to make it legally binding and uncontestable.

Living will: It includes instructions on how to use or refrain from using any and all extraordinary life-sustaining efforts. In California, this would fall under the Advance Health Care Directive.

Life insurance: He has multiple policies with multiple beneficiaries, including parents, siblings, long-time family servants, and a few elderly female relatives.

Retirement accounts: All are set to roll over into trust funds to support the educational efforts of all subsequent generations of nieces and nephews if they achieve specific GPAs. Financial rewards go to those who exceed those levels.

Living trust: Dividends are spent every month on lavish parties, resort vacations, and redoing the summer house in the Hamptons.

Charitable remainder trust: Several specific charities get what is left over, which will be about $11 million.

Social security: Benefits will go to support arts organizations.

Maya E. Primwater

Will: 50 percent of everything not in a trust goes to John. The will has just enough information to make it legally binding and uncontestable.

Living will: Has instructions not to use extraordinary life-sustaining efforts.

Life insurance: She has multiple policies with multiple beneficiaries, including siblings, lifelong friends, and charities.

Retirement accounts: All are set to roll over into an endowment fund to provide ongoing support for more than two dozen charities and nonprofits for which Maya volunteers.

Living trust: Dividends are spent every month on visits to overseas non-profit organizations doing research for her endowment.

Education trust funds: Several funds are set up to send her nieces and nephews, cousins, and the children of close friends to study abroad; other funds are set up for independent study for those who want to find their way in a less academic environment.

Social security: Benefits will go to support local social justice groups.

Whatever money is left in her retirement accounts is to be placed in trust after her death to establish a writers' retreat the Write on the Sound Writer's Conference will operate.

• *Did You Know?* •

The person who will eventually administer your estate has some basic guidelines to follow due to state and federal laws. Specific taxes must be paid by certain deadlines. An extension could be granted if the paperwork were completed in a certain way, submitted to the correct office, and signed by a specific person or judge. You can help make this process flow a little more smoothly by keeping that in mind and planning for some potential problems.

☑ Watch Out for This

☐ Prepare a letter with details about how to administer your estate.

☐ Provide as much detailed information as possible about your estate. Annual updates to your documents will mean fewer undocumented items for the executor to track down.

☐ Bonding requirements for your executor can be waived if you include language in your will to that effect. If your executor is a bank, you might want to keep those in place, but for a family member, this might not be necessary.

☐ The court requires with probate proceedings death notices to heirs and creditors. To make it easier, provide a list of your known relatives and creditors for your executor.

Your executor should be aware of the following items:

☐ Publish the death notices properly to avoid disputes.

☐ Be diligent in identifying and inventorying assets; an apparent lack of effort can result in legal trouble.

☐ Ask questions about anything that is unclear in legal documents and estate administration instructions, and get clarification in writing. This can help avoid potential disputes or help address those that do arise.

Details neither of you control:

☐ Disputes creditors raise or dissatisfaction about how a claim is settled.

☐ Disagreements between beneficiaries and challenges they bring up.

☐ A spouse's claims against an estate that conflict with the terms of a will; some states entitle a spouse to a specific percentage of an estate regardless of the decedent's wishes.

CASE STUDY: COMPONENTS OF AN EFFECTIVE ESTATE PLAN

Anne Marie Griffith, Tom Kotick
SS&G Financial Services Inc.
Certified Public Accountants and
Advisers
tkotick@ssandg.com

What is essential to include in an estate plan?

Estate planning is the process of developing and implementing a master plan that facilitates the distribution of your property after your death according to your goals and objectives.

The critical pieces of estate planning involve the following documents: a will; a trust in the case of minor children, a large estate, or second marriage with children from prior marriages; durable powers of attorney; and a living will and a medical power of attorney or medical proxy. A letter of instructions is also recommended.

Other critical priorities of the estate-planning process involve the selection of an executor/executrix for your will/estate, a guardian for your minor children, and trustees or co-trustees in the case of any trusts created. Finally, a cash-flow analysis and some income tax planning should be part of the estate-planning priority list.

Anyone with property or minor children should have a will. Although most people think of the will as the driving factor determining where your property goes, beneficiary designations and the titling of assets often play a bigger role in this determination. For example, when someone owns property as joint tenants with rights of survivorship, this property will go to the joint owner regardless of what a will says. Also, beneficiary designations govern many assets, such as retirement plans and life insurance. These types of assets will always pass by way of the beneficiary designation, not according to a person's will.

Life insurance is one of the biggest players in the estate-planning game. For some, it is the only way to ensure family members will be able to support themselves after the death of the primary wage earner. For those with larger estates, life insurance can provide the funds needed to pay estate taxes and other costs without liquidating estate assets. For those with a business interest, life insurance can be used as a vehicle for business succession. Finally, for those with a generous spirit, life insurance can permit you to make charitable gifts.

What are the most common mistakes people make? What do people forget to include?

A common mistake is not addressing the estate-planning process at all, which can result in what is called dying intestate, or dying without a will. In that case, the state resolves the distribution of the estate and the care of minor children.

Another oversight is not funding the estate to properly care for your spouse or your minor or school-aged children in terms of daily living expenses and future educational costs.

Other common mistakes or oversights are in the need for annual income tax filings for any trusts that have been created, or gift-tax return filings in the case of gifts over the annual exclusion amount.

What are the benefits of working with someone in your field?

A CPA who is experienced in working with clients on their personal financial plans, which include estate planning, can help avoid the mistakes and oversights mentioned previously.

The CPA can effectuate the "quarterbacking" of the estate-planning process. This is done in several ways. One is helping the attorney draft the documents according to the client's needs and desires and recommending a good estate attorney if the client does not enter the process with an attorney. Another is coordinating the work of the investment broker to properly identify and retitle assets. Working with the life insurance agent to make sure ongoing living and education expenses are covered with the right amount and type of life insurance coverage and policy is another.

The CPA is usually involved in preparing any annual trust or gift-tax filing requirements that might spring from the planning process. The CPA will gather the information necessary to make the filings by coordinating the assistance and necessary input from the other team members to make the proper filings each year.

How does a person go about choosing a professional in your field?

If a client is working with a CPA for his annual personal and business accounting and tax work, he can start by asking if the CPA does income taxes and estate planning. Or he could ask his CPA for a referral to a CPA who is experienced in the financial aspects of estate planning.

Additional certifications, such as the PFS (Personal Financial Specialist) designation or a CFP® (Certified Financial Planner®), help qualify the CPA. Also helpful is a CPA who has studied for and retains a state life insurance license.

USA, California, Los Angeles, downtown and freeway interchange

CHAPTER 4

Taxes

When Roman Emperor Caesar Augustus was running short on cash to pay for aqueducts and parties, he created the first estate levy. Ever since then, death and taxes have been linked. Our version of that original tax law has become complicated and confusing over time.

When one loophole is discovered, a new rule is created to cover it. Then, that rule has a little wiggle room, so another rule is created, and the cycle continues. Do not count on an easy answer to the question of how much tax money your estate will have to pay after you die. Your best bet is to track down people who specialize in tax law: a CPA or an attorney.

The gross estate, which is the value of all property the deceased person owns on the date of death, is what gets taxed. The federal government gets an estate tax based on the Estate Recovery Act. Those in Congress who want to completely do away with it refer to it as the death tax. Some states have an estate tax similar to that of the federal government, though other states levy an inheritance tax on the property the beneficiary receives. All these taxes have a host of exemptions or deductions that reduce or eliminate the taxes that need to be paid.

California does not presently require an estate tax. California might change this when the federal tax scheme changes. Taxes are never a constant. Tax changes at both federal and state levels are one of the main reasons for updating estate plans.

When taxes are an issue, strategically using the exemptions and deductions and also creating tax-free accounts makes it possible to get around some of these taxes. That is one of the best benefits of estate planning. Before you can save taxes, you need to know what they are and how much you might owe. Without a crystal ball or clairvoyance, it is impossible to know what the precise worth of your estate will be at the time of your death or the tax scheme that will affect it, but planning for what you do know puts you in a position to help your loved ones avoid some painful tax bills.

Keep in mind no matter how much you prepare, the tax laws can be changed with the stroke of a pen in Washington, D.C., or Sacramento, Calfornia, and everything you thought you knew and planned for can be changed. Consider all the information in this section subject to change at any time; do not consider this information to be the definitive legal authority.

Check with a tax professional who is current with federal and state tax law changes.

Federal First

Three federal taxes could affect your estate: the gift tax, the generation-skipping transfer tax, and the estate tax.

Any gift, cash or property transfer, you give to another person in one fiscal year is subject to a gift tax. There is one exemption: The first $13,000 given to any single person or organization is exempt from the tax, but everything from $13,001 and beyond is subject to taxation.

▶ *Example:* You decide to give your niece Meghan $5,000 as a high school graduation present because she wants to tour Europe before going to college.

Do you owe? No. Because this gift is under $13,000, you do not owe any taxes on this gift. But you can only give Meghan another $8,000 this year without paying taxes. If you make the next gift $9,000, you will owe the gift tax on $1,000.

As the donor, the person who gives a gift, you are eligible for some tax deductions that might also make the tax bill go away. The donee, the person or institution receiving the gift, is what determines the deduction or exclusion you can apply: gifts to your spouse and many charities receive deductions and gifts related to medical expenses, political organizations, and tuition receive exlusions.

▶ *Example:* Your husband has an opportunity to buy a workshop full of woodworking tools from an elderly neighbor who is giving up the hobby. He has his own checking account, but it was his turn to add money to the children's college fund this month, and he does not have enough cash. You give him the money from your checking account.

Do you owe? No. The marital tax deduction allows you to give your spouse $150,000 in a year, and it is tax-free. But if you try to do the same thing for the man you have lived with for 18 years and are not married to, you will have to pay the gift tax on $137,000. You still get to take advantage of the annual $13,000 exemption.

Like most things, these deductions and exclusions all have fine print. To have a tax-free marital deduction, you must be married and your spouse must be a U.S. citizen at the time you make the gift.

▶ *Example:* It is Friday night, and your grandson Thomas calls. He sounds absolutely frantic. His tuition is due the following week, and he *cannot reach Mom, who is out of state at a convention. Dad has not been around for years, and even if he were, he almost certainly would not have the $13,200 your grandson owes. You write down the name of the school, address, and all of the particulars so you can have your bank transfer the funds on Monday.*

Do you owe? No. For the education exclusion to apply, the gift must be paid directly to the educational institution so you will not owe any taxes. But the education exclusion is for tuition or training only. Thomas is on his own for books unless you give him additional cash.

When it comes to charities, the Internal Revenue Service (IRS) must qualify them. You cannot just give money to an animal shelter and deduct that from your taxes; you have to make sure the IRS has decided it is a charity, and the gifts you give to a charity need to fit into predetermined categories:

- **Charitable gift:** This is property that you give to a charity without getting anything in return. The gift can be cash or any other type of property.

- **Bargain sale:** This is the sale of a piece of property to a charity at a rate that is below the fair market value. The difference between the amount paid and the actual value is the amount of the gift.

- **Stock bailout:** The transfer of stock ownership from your name to that of the charity. The fair market value of the stock at the time of the transfer is the gift amount.

Many other conditions must be met to make your gift tax-free regardless of who gets the gift. That is why you must consult with a tax expert to make sure your interpretation of your gift matches what the government allows.

Unless you are a whiz at tax law, you are probably going to need help navigating the ever changing federal estate tax.

In 2001, a law called the Economic Growth and Tax Relief Reconciliation Act was passed that increased the exemption for the estate tax. In 2002 and 2003, taxes were owed on anything more than $1 million. So if your estate was worth $1.5 million, you only had to pay tax on $500,000. At a 45 percent tax rate — the highest federal tax rate for an estate — the exemptions create a limit to the money the feds can collect. The exemption increased to $3.5 million until 2009, then the tax was repealed in 2010 until 2011, when the exemption went back down to $1 million.

Some people managed to dodge the estate tax dilemma. A person with a multimillion-dollar estate did not want to have less money to give to her beneficiaries, so she named her grandchildren or great-grandchildren as the beneficiaries. They are all minors, so they do not have to pay any taxes on their inheritance. But the federal government caught on to that and specifically taxes the money skipping generations. Called the Generation-Skipping Tax Transfer (GSTT), it is the most complex tax law, according to the experts in the field.

Entire books are written about this topic that do not encompass all the details. If your estate is worth more than $2 million, you will want to work with an estate-tax planner to make sure you look at the implications of trying to give all your goods to the youngest in your family tree.

• *Did You Know?* •

Children under the age of 14 are required to pay income tax at the rate for single filers on income earned through employment. They must file a tax return like everyone else, but they get special treatment by the IRS if their parents are wealthy and try to give a large sum of money.

"Kiddie tax" is the term used to describe income tax applied to money that minors did not earn through employment, also called unearned income. In 1996, a special law was created to close a loophole that allowed parents to give their children a large gift as a way to pay a lower tax on the interest they earned. The child tax rate was significantly lower than the adult rate.

The law has changed over the years, and in 2008, it changed again. The first $1,000 in income made on any investment in the name of a child 19 and younger or 24 and younger if the child is in school full time is not subject to income tax. The next $1,000 is subject to a 10 percent tax. Anything above $2,000 is taxed at the tax rate of the child's parent(s).

☑ Watch Out for This

☐ You can take advantage of your child's lower income-tax bracket by investing in U.S. Savings Bonds. The income is deferred, and so are the taxes.

☐ Money paid to your child in the form of wages for working in your business is not subject to the kiddie tax. Those payments are deductible by your business, but it is important to keep the necessary records for hours and work performed. Not having these could make it appear as though you are trying to cheat on your business taxes.

☐ A child earning her own income and paying taxes can still be declared as a dependent on a parent's tax return, which allows that parent to take a standard deduction. If you divorce and do not get custody of the children, you can not use the standard deduction for your taxes.

Now for the State

The state wants to get some of that estate you are leaving behind, too. Some copied the federal law and have created a state estate tax, which means your estate has to pay taxes on the property you leave behind. Because these taxes are tied to the federal tax, you need to make sure you are looking at the most current federal estate-tax tables to know the amount the California estate tax will be if and when it applies.

Other states levy an inheritance tax on the property a beneficiary receives. California does not presently have an inheritance tax. The structure of these taxes depend on the state law, but as a rule, the closer the relationship the beneficiary has to the deceased, the lower his tax will be. For example, a brother will have a larger exemption and a lower tax rate than a distant cousin.

Some states also impose a state gift tax. California does not. To find out whether your state has such a tax and whether there is an annual exclusion, lifetime exemptions for close family members, or other legal technicalities, a good place to begin is the state's department of revenue or an equivalent.

Then, there is the state income tax. Tax on income earned during a fiscal year is for residents of that state. You can be a full- or part-time resident or simply live in the state for a few months out of the year but not officially be registered as a part-time resident. Income earned in another state might be taxable in California.

Finally, some states also tax on intangible property, such as bonds, stocks, accounts receivable, and patents. This also is not currently a state tax in California. In some states, though, giving any of those things from your estate to a family member or friend before or after you die could result in a tax for the recipient.

Mistakes Happen... Frequently

The only federal regulation that might be more complex than tax law is immigration law. This complexity is why people make costly mistakes, miss savings opportunities, and get confused about what can and cannot be done legally. Most tax specialists are CPAs or lawyers, and it is their job to stay ahead of the latest changes to the growing tax code.

Over time, some common mistakes related to taxes and estate planning have emerged. This list is a sample of those errors; they can help you identify holes in your own planning, help you prepare for a meeting with a tax advisor, and at least inspire you not to get careless about managing this element of your own estate plan.

Mistakes your executor could make include:

- Using the wrong IRS forms when filing taxes. This could include consulting the wrong tables and filling out and submitting the wrong schedule, such as using the 1040 EZ income tax form when by law you are required to use the 1040 long form.

- Omitting information about your estate. If you do not provide or disclose all the information, your executor might not know about an account that is taxable, which makes him or her liable for any oversight that occurs. Claiming ignorance will not work as a defense.

- Not having the necessary record to justify or back up the filing. This could include having no mileage record and missing receipts and account interest statements.

- Preparing a return without professional help. Professionals who are updated on all the current tax laws can help an executor avoid a multitude of mistakes, such as using the wrong form or having insufficient documentation.

- Miscalculating. This could include transposing numbers or just coming up with the wrong number when adding or subtracting.

- Not signing the tax form.

Avoid mistakes when making the following decisions for an estate plan:

- When to bequeath a gift: before or after death

- How to use gifts that fall below the annual gift tax exclusion amount, which was $14,000 in 2015

- The most advantageous way to structure a life insurance policy

- Which trust will have the maximum tax advantages for you and the beneficiary

- When it is best to leave property to a spouse

- Whether to make a bequest that will negatively impact the tax position of the beneficiary

If you want to look up a specific topic or try your hand at sorting the rules related to a specific estate-planning element, such as trusts, refer to **www.irs.gov**.

When, Not If, You Pay

The No. 1 benefit of estate planning many professionals cite is dramatic reduction in the amount of taxes that will be paid out of your estate. However, the only way to accomplish that is to know the tax laws of California, the tax requirements of any state in which you own property, and the tax implications of the way you choose to save and distribute your estate.

There are some helpful details to know about taxes when doing your estate planning:

The federal estate tax rate has ranged from 45 to 50 percent. It is best to check where those rates stand every time you review or change your estate plan. Make sure you have enough money available to cover the bill if you do not want your loved ones to have to pay. You could put a provision in your will to pick up any taxes for your beneficiaries if you wanted to, but a lawyer is going to have to help you with the wording to make that possible.

It is the job of the executor of your estate to handle all these money matters. In addition to calculating the value of your estate, she must file a tax return for your estate, called the fiduciary return, with the IRS and make the necessary payments, if there are any.

There will be a deadline for paying an estate tax. That deadline is generally 90 days after the date of death, but sometimes arrangements can be made for special circumstances.

Generally, the best way to avoid or minimize taxes is to leave your entire estate to your spouse, a charity, or some combination of those two or set up a trust. This is not an area in which to guess. Your executor likely will have a few options for saving some tax money, but advance advice from an estate-planning professional is crucial. Also, if your executor does the wrong thing, it could cost him or her personally. Your executor should consider the following:

- Be sure all possible deductions are included in the fiduciary return; these include funeral expenses, expenses to your estate, such as appraisal fees or probate court costs; debts, such as mortgage or credit cards; charitable contributions; and marital deductions. The marital deduction can only be taken if your spouse is a U.S. citizen.

- Value the assets of the estate at a later date instead of right at death. This can only be done under the correct circumstances, and whether it is beneficial depends upon the individual estate and time of death.

- Income going into the estate can be manipulated to the advantage of the estate. Schedule the sale of property or acceptance of payments due at a time advantageous to filing the deceased's last income tax return and the fiduciary return for the estate.

- Estate distributions to beneficiaries can also be timed so the beneficiary must pay the tax, not the estate. If the payments to beneficiaries are made before the fiduciary return is filed, the estate's value drops and the taxes due also drop.

Your beneficiaries can also reduce their tax bills by declining to accept a bequest. Federal and state tax laws permit a disclaimer, which is a refusal to accept a gift. Whether this is a single beneficiary or joint bequest, one or both parties can decline, but it must be refused in writing commonly within nine months of your death.

There are choices you can make in your estate planning before others need to make decisions about how to handle the taxes on your estate. When properly coordinated, some choices create an opportunity to reduce the potential tax burden on your estate and beneficiaries. These are some ways to reduce taxes, so keep these in mind when working on your estate plan:

- Make gifts before you die to reduce your estate's value.

- Put property into tax-free trusts. *See Chapter 6 for more information about your choices.*

- Schedule property transfers to take place at the time of your death.

- Coordinate your estate planning with your spouse and divvy up assets to the best advantage of both of you.

- Use permissible exemptions, such as leaving your entire estate to your spouse.

- Consider investing in life insurance and structuring the policies carefully. *See Chapter 7 for more information on how this works.*

However, like all estate-planning decisions, choosing the wrong options or not using the right language can waste all your careful planning. Do not try this on your own.

• *Did You Know?* •

The fees paid to an executor as compensation for the time she puts into managing and closing out your estate are taxable income. If your executor opts not to accept a fee, the money you designate for that purpose becomes part of your estate. If it is not held in a tax-free account, that money can be subject to estate tax.

☑ Watch Out for This

☐ Talk to your executor about a fee. If he does not want to be compensated, you can plan accordingly.

CASE STUDY: TAX ADVICE FROM THE IRS

Internal Revenue Service (IRS)
1-800-829-1040
Hours of operation: Monday - Friday,
7 a.m. - 10 p.m. your local time
(Alaska & Hawaii follow Pacific Time)
www.irs.gov

The IRS is the ultimate source for all things related to taxes. Its website offers extensive resources for those who wish to learn more about taxes. What follows is a copy of the frequently asked questions on the Estate Taxes page. The IRS is not in the habit of helping people figure out how to reduce their tax bills, but they will give you all you need to know to be legal. Simply achieving the goal of compliance with tax law is not something even the FAQ can guarantee. The recurring qualifiers and other sources you need to check make it clear that dealing with estate taxes on your own is risky.

When can I expect the Estate Tax Closing Letter?

There can be some variation, but for returns that are accepted as filed and contain no other errors or special circumstances, you should expect to wait about four to six months after filing to receive your closing letter. Returns that are selected for examination or reviewed for statistical purposes will take longer.

What is included in the estate?

The gross estate of the decedent consists of an accounting of everything you own or have certain interests in at the date of death. The fair market value of these items, not necessarily what you paid for them or what their values were when you acquired them, is used. The total of all of these items is your gross estate. The includible property might consist of cash and securities, real estate, insurance, trusts, annuities, business interests, and other assets. Keep in mind the gross estate will likely include nonprobate as well as probate property.

I own a half interest in a farm, building, or business with another person. What is included?

Depending on how your half interest is held and treated under state law and how it was acquired, you would probably only include half of its value in your gross estate. However, many other factors influence this answer, so you would need to visit with a tax or legal professional to make that determination.

What is excluded from the estate?

Generally, the gross estate does not include property owned solely by the decedent's spouse or other individuals. Lifetime gifts that are complete with no retention of powers or other control are not included in the gross estate. Taxable gifts are used in the computation of the estate tax. Life estates given to the decedent by others in which the decedent has no further control or power at the date of death are not included.

Which deductions reduce the estate tax?

1. Marital deduction: One of the primary deductions for married decedents is the marital deduction. All property that is included in the gross estate and passes to the surviving spouse is eligible. The property must pass outright. In some cases, certain life estates also qualify for the marital deduction.

2. Charitable deduction: If the decedent leaves property to a qualifying charity, it can be deducted from the gross estate.

3. Mortgages and debt

4. Administration expenses of the estate

5. Losses during estate administration

What other information do I need to include with the return?
Among other items listed:

1. Copies of the death certificate

2. Copies of the decedent's will and relevant trusts

3. Copies of appraisals

4. Copies of documents relevant to litigation involving the estate

5. Documentation of any unusual items shown on the return, such as partially included assets, losses, transfers near the date of death, and others

What is "fair market value?"

Fair market value is defined as "the price at which the property would change hands between a willing buyer and a willing seller, neither being under any compulsion to buy or to sell, and both having reasonable knowledge of relevant facts. The fair market value of a particular item of property includible in the decedent's gross estate is not to be determined by a forced sale price. Nor is the fair market value of an item of property to be determined by the sale price of the item in a market other than that in which such item is most commonly sold to the public, taking into account the location of the item wherever appropriate."

What about the values of my family business and farm?

Generally, the fair market value of such interests the decedent owned are includible in the gross estate at date of death. However, for certain farms or businesses operated as a family farm or business, reductions to these amounts might be available.

In the case of a qualifying family farm, IRC §2032A allows a reduction from value of up to $820,000.

If the decedent owned an interest in a qualifying family-owned business, a deduction from the gross estate in the amount of up to $1,100,000 might be available under IRC §2057.

What if I do not have everything ready for filing by the due date?

The estate's representative can request an extension of time to file for up to six months from the due date of the return. However, the correct amount of tax is still due by the due date, and interest is accrued on any amounts still owed by the due date that are not paid at that time.

Whom should I hire to represent me and file the return?

The IRS cannot make recommendations about specific individuals, but consider several factors:

1. How complex is the estate? By the time most estates reach $1,000,000, there is usually some complexity involved.
2. How large is the estate?
3. In what condition are the decedent's records?
4. How many beneficiaries are there, and are they cooperative?
5. Do I need an attorney, CPA, enrolled agent (EA), or other professional(s)?

With these questions in mind, it is a good idea to discuss the matter with several attorneys and CPAs or EAs. Ask how much experience they have had, and ask for referrals. This process should be similar to locating a good physician. Locate other individuals who have had similar experiences and ask for recommendations. Finally, after the representative has begun to work on estate matters, make sure the lines of communication remain open so there are no surprises during administration or if the estate tax return is examined.

Finally, most estates engage the services of both attorneys and CPAs or EAs. The attorney usually handles probate matters and reviews the impact of documents on the estate tax return. The CPA or EA often handles the actual return preparation and some representation of the estate in matters with the IRS. However, some attorneys handle all the work. CPAs and EAs can also handle most of the work but cannot take care of probate matters and other situations in which a law license is required. In addition, other professionals, such as appraisers, surveyors, financial advisors, and others, might need to be engaged during this time.

Do I have to talk to the IRS during an examination?

You do not have to be present during an examination unless an IRS representative needs to ask specific questions. Although you can represent yourself during an examination, most executors prefer the professional they employed to handle this phase of administration. They can delegate authority for this by signing a designation on the Form 706 itself, or executing Form 2848, "Power of Attorney."

What if I disagree with the examination proposals?

You have many rights and avenues of appeal if you disagree with any proposals the IRS mad.

What happens if I sell property that I have inherited?

The sale of such property is usually considered the sale of a capital asset and might be subject to capital gains or loss treatment. However, IRC §1014 provides that the basis of property acquired from a decedent is its fair market value at the date of death, so there is usually little or no gain to account for if the sale occurs soon after the date of death. Remember, the rules are different for determining the basis of property received as a lifetime gift.

Death is Big Business for the Federal Government

The federal government is the first beneficiary to get a share of your or any estate. The IRS keeps statistics including the number of deaths by state, the number of estates that pay taxes, and the amount of taxes paid. Part of that information is listed below to give you a sense of just how much money was added to the coffers of the U.S. government.

These numbers are in the thousands of dollars. After you add the zeros, you might find new motivation for planning now so your family does not have to pay later.

Statistic of Income (SOI) Estate Tax Data Tables, Selected Years of Death

The data included in these SOI tables are for returns filed for decedents who died in the same year and whose estates would have been subject to the same tax law and similar economic conditions.

Note: These numbers are for illustrative purpose and predate the estate tax law's 2010 limbo status.

Estate Tax Returns Filed in 2013 [1], by State of Residence

All figures are estimates based on a sample--money amounts are in thousands of dollars.

State of Residence	Gross estate, tax purposes		Net estate tax	
	Number	Amount	Number	Amount
Total	10,568	138,704,642	4,687	12,666,774
Alabama	88	1,611,422	44	141,607
Alaska	* 13	* 229,422	d	d
Arizona	129	1,461,581	53	91,332
Arkansas	74	680,833	26	68,722
California	1,766	25,218,125	838	2,605,207
Colorado	158	1,697,031	90	161,590
Connecticut	277	3,848,258	124	435,580
Delaware	* 12	* 122,399	* 8	* 11,125
District of Columbia	62	735,302	39	47,498
Florida	1,240	19,698,209	569	2,316,746
Georgia	191	2,020,871	83	134,525
Hawaii	36	376,262	22	40,090
Idaho	33	297,145	* 16	* 26,110
Illinois	540	5,458,257	193	329,648
Indiana	105	1,442,493	48	132,894
Iowa	157	1,270,059	53	79,786
Kansas	97	1,167,057	37	84,012
Kentucky	76	1,465,935	39	160,837
Louisiana	120	1,220,562	73	136,222
Maine	32	543,487	d	d
Maryland	158	2,025,609	65	160,994
Massachusetts	273	3,132,257	121	297,910
Michigan	189	2,306,800	84	173,813
Minnesota	178	1,847,084	49	128,325
Mississippi	51	601,462	26	51,058
Missouri	191	2,181,572	81	202,081
Montana	38	319,360	* 19	* 7,588
Nebraska	97	1,277,442	52	98,966
Nevada	81	921,192	28	55,398

State of Residence	Gross estate, tax purposes		Net estate tax	
	Number	Amount	Number	Amount
New Hampshire	49	703,263	16	81,818
New Jersey	351	3,573,309	111	225,278
New Mexico	43	501,338	24	37,758
New York	907	15,476,544	370	933,389
North Carolina	200	2,119,905	100	157,049
North Dakota	32	263,590	* 19	* 23,684
Ohio	223	3,066,691	89	531,425
Oklahoma	103	1,306,797	42	56,153
Oregon	114	1,168,354	46	78,485
Pennsylvania	350	5,063,982	141	539,384
Rhode Island	25	258,444	* 19	* 27,700
South Carolina	96	1,061,234	51	108,280
South Dakota	32	429,544	* 17	* 20,533
Tennessee	125	1,352,107	51	132,956
Texas	683	8,413,545	292	757,724
Utah	59	674,659	27	58,925
Vermont	32	203,178	* 15	* 3,279
Virginia	266	3,271,190	174	295,616
Washington	200	2,302,131	86	136,678
West Virginia	18	222,616	* 11	* 21,640
Wisconsin	136	1,302,692	63	126,685
Wyoming	10	245,997	d	d
Other areas [2]	52	546,048	35	40,081

NOTE: Detail might not add to total because of rounding.

* *Estimates should be used with caution because of the small number of sample returns on which they were based.*

[1] Generally, an estate files a Federal estate tax return (Form 706) in the year after a decedent's death. So, in 2013, most returns were filed for deaths that occurred in 2012, for which the filing threshold was $5.12 million. Because of filing extensions, however, some returns were filed in 2013 for deaths that occurred prior to 2012, for which filing thresholds were lower.

[2] Includes U.S. territories, U.S. citizens domiciled abroad, and a small number of returns for whom State of residence was unknown.

Source: IRS, Statistics of Income Division, Estate Tax Returns Study, October 2014.

Union Station, Los Angeles, California, USA

CHAPTER 5
Wills

A family, dressed entirely in black, sits around grandpa's book-lined study and fidgets while the elderly lawyer sitting behind the leather-topped desk cleans his glasses and clears his throat before rasping, "Being of sound mind and body…" The scene is pure Hollywood, but most lawyers will tell you to save the drama for personal letters and keep your will legally correct to avoid potential problems. Make sure beneficiaries know what they are getting so your family can be at home and not in a lawyer's office getting tied up in more drama the day after the funeral.

A will is a legal document that identifies which people or institutions receive money and property from your estate after your death. It also serves to appoint guardianship of children or adults who are your legal responsibility and designates an executor to manage your estate after you die. With standard will forms available on the Internet, preparing a will would seem easy. But choosing the wrong kind of will, not having enough witnesses, leaving out key language required in California, or having inadequate particulars can mean the state, not you, will decide what happens to your estate.

Will substitutes, such as a living trust, can accomplish many of the things a will is designed to do, but it is still a good idea to have a will in addition to other estate-planning options because the state imposes a will on you if you do not write one of your own. If you die and leave possessions behind, someone has to divvy them up, and the state assumes that responsibility if you do not do a good job of it.

When you die, if you have a valid will, you die "testate." If you do not have a will when you die, you are intestate, and laws in California determine what happens to your belongings. The legal system will distribute your assets, not you. Because your debts have to be paid when you die, including federal and state taxes, your creditors are paid first, and then your beneficiaries will get what is left over.

Most experts will tell you having a will prepared by a lawyer is worth the investment of time and money for the safety and protection it provides. But before you can ask about one, you need to know what goes into a will.

Will Basics

To make sure your will is legal and can be executed, some essential information is necessary. Using your legal name in your will — the one that is on your birth certificate and under which you file your tax returns — makes it harder for a person, the state, or an institution to challenge your will.

Because you are a resident, California will have jurisdiction over your will. After you die, your will is submitted to probate court. The address listed in your will should be in the state in which you vote, hold a driver's license, and have your primary residence. Documentation is necessary to prove the state in which you live.

Another important point about where you live is whether your state has a community property law on the books. If so, whatever property falls into your state's definition of community property will be jointly owned by a wife and a husband, which potentially limits what you can do with that property in your will.

One more state-related issue is ownership of property outside California. If you live in California but own a condo in another state, the California probate court will not directly handle the out-of-state property. The court in the state where the property is located will oversee the transition of ownership. When preparing your will, you need to take this into account. Just because you own it does not mean you get to control what happens to it after your death.

Wills Defined

The will that most people think of, called a simple will, is a legal document that applies to only one person. But all wills, to be legal, need to include a number of elements. The will needs to identify who you are, your beneficiaries, your executor, the directions you leave for the care of people for whom you are responsible, and the distribution of your assets.

These are basic elements every will needs to have:

- **Beneficiary:** The individual(s) or group(s) who will receive the property.

- **Executor:** Also called a personal representative, this is the individual who handles the property you are leaving behind. If you die without a will, the court appoints an administrator, frequently a spouse or adult child, who will serve in the same capacity by handling all the paperwork, preparing assets, dealing with likely heirs, handling claims from creditors, making payments on outstanding debt, and resolving other estate-related matters.

- **Clauses:** The sections in your will that likely organize the information in a specific order.

    o **Opening clauses:** Lay out the basic information about who you are and set the stage for the clauses that follow:

▶ The **introductory clause** *identifies you as the person who is making the will.*

▶ The **family-statement clause** *introduces and identifies the family members who will be referred to later in the will.*

▶ The **tax clause** *explains how the taxes of your estate will be paid.*

o **Survival clause:** This leaves everything in your estate to one named person. Married people frequently do this to ensure everything goes to the surviving spouse.

o **Guardianship clause:** The appointment of a guardian for children under the age of 18 is handled in this clause. A successor guardian should also be named as a backup.

o **Giving clauses:** These clauses leave specific bequests, or property that is identified by name and description, to beneficiaries and explain which property goes to which person and under which circumstances. These can be as broad or explicit as you want. They are divided according to the following categories:

▶ **Real property clauses:** *Statements that match up property with a person. For example, you want your spouse, Susan, to have the house and your brother, Fred, to have your antique baseball card collection.*

▶ **Personal property clauses:** *Use these when you want to be explicit in your instructions. For example, you want Teddy to get the Google stock and Elizabeth gets the General Motors stock.*

o **Residuary clause, or residue:** Addresses the parts of your estate that you do not detail in a specific clause. The residuary clause is essential for any kind of will to make sure anything you forget or might have acquired after the will was prepared can be distributed. Naming at least one beneficiary is good for keeping your assets out of the hands of the courts; naming two or more alternative beneficiaries is better. For example, you want Bertha Jones, your second cousin twice removed, and her husband, Bubba Jones, to benefit from what is not given to anyone else. If either or both of them predeceases you, all of the balance of your estate goes to Bubba Jones Jr.

o **Appointment clause:** Identifies the person who will manage your estate. For example, Robert Anthony, your best friend since college, will serve as the executor of your estate.

o **Fiduciary powers clause:** The language that gives your executor the power to serve as your executor and perform any duties that go beyond the basic requirements in California regulations. For example, Robert Anthony will have the ability to provide your spouse, children, and parents with income until your estate is settled.

o **Ending clauses:** These include the legalities to meet statutory requirements so your will is legal and valid, which include, but are not limited to, your signature, date, location of the signing, and witnesses.

Your will can be as broad or specific as you choose. As one piece of your overall estate plan, your will should be seen as one of several tools and prepared accordingly.

If you wanted to keep your affairs private, a more broad will would be in order. Once a will is entered in California probate court, anyone can read it because it becomes a public record. If you have seen the children of a deceased friend get into fistfights over a couch or go to court over an offshore investment account, you might want to go into more detail.

There are different kinds of wills from which to choose to meet your specific needs. The format of these wills changes depending on who is represented in the will, what the will is designed to do, and how it is prepared.

Tips for Creating Your Will

Essentials elements for a valid will include:

- Recorded in writing. Wills that are given verbally might not stand up in court.
- Your name and age
- "Being of sound mind." This means you know the property in your possession and the people or institutions identified as beneficiaries.
- Clearly stated and intended to transfer property
- Signed voluntarily
- Witnessed properly
- Executed properly. The will must include a statement that attests to the fact that this is your will, the date, the place it is signed, and witnesses.

Mistakes to avoid in your will include:

- Making dramatic personal statements that have nothing to do with the distribution of property and can end up creating confusion
- Not being specific enough. If language is ambiguous, it is subject to interpretation, and the court makes the final ruling.
- Not asking someone to be your executor or take power-of-attorney responsibilities
- Left over and not enough property to meet the conditions of your will
- Using beneficiaries as witnesses who sign the will. You want to avoid the potential appearance of a conflict of interest and undue influence over the person making the will.
- Making many changes at once or over time and not creating a new will. Excessive changes can lead to confusion.

The original document

If the original will is stored in a safe deposit box, it could become inaccessible after your death if that box is in your name only. Have your lawyer retain the original will in his or her files so it is readily accessible.

Other will-related documents

Your original durable power of attorney, medical power of attorney, living will, and any other documents related to incapacitation should also be stored in your lawyer's office. Those taking responsibility for making medical, financial, or other decisions should have a copy of that power of attorney.

Copies

Keeping your will private is a decision you will need to make based on a conversation with your lawyer. Unusual clauses or issues might warrant making copies of the documents and sharing them with key people in advance so nobody is surprised when the will is executed. Your wishes regarding what should happen if you were to become incapacitated and who is responsible for making decisions on your behalf should be shared with all family members and close friends. This way, there can be no question about what you would like done.

Do not sign copies of a will, or it might qualify as a legal duplicate original. Write COPY in ink on each page to make sure nobody can claim a copy is the original.

Especially in the cases of serious illness and a do-not-resuscitate (DNR) order, a living will, and organ donation, your physicians and other medical providers need to have copies. Your doctors might have their own form for you to fill out related to these matters; be sure to check.

The "who" of a will

Mutual will: This is a plan for your estate that is prepared in conjunction with another person.

▶ *Example: Sisters Carol and Angie agree to support their disabled brother, Brian, and Grandma Jane. They decide no matter who dies first, 40 percent of either estate goes to Brian, 40 percent goes to Grandma Jane, and the remaining 20 percent goes to other beneficiaries. When the other person dies, 50 percent of her estate goes to Brian,*

20 percent goes to Grandma Jane, and the remaining 30 percent goes to other beneficiaries. If Grandma Jane dies before Carol or Angie, her portion goes to Brian.

Joint will: This is one legal document for any two people, such as you and your spouse. The problem with this kind of will is that it is irrevocable. It cannot be changed after one of the two parties dies because both people must make all decisions. A lawyer can tell you when this kind of will is a good idea, but most suggest separate wills to avoid complications. Furthermore, because joint wills are not specifically referenced in the California Probate Code, you should not attempt a joint will approach without consulting a California lawyer.

Simple will: A single legal document written by one person that identifies who you are, your beneficiaries, your executor, the directions you leave for the care of people for whom you are responsible, and the distribution of your assets.

The "what" of a will

Pour-over will: This will place some property into a trust that was established while you were still alive.

Testamentary trust will: This will move your assets into one or more trusts after your death. *See Chapter 6 for more information on trusts.*

The "how" of a will

Holographic will: This is a handwritten document you sign but is not witnessed by anyone else. Some states recognize a handwritten will as valid, but California does not recognize holographic wills. *See Chapter 11 for more information on how this works in California.*

• *Did You Know?* •

Federal and state law typically define children as the biological offspring of a heterosexual couple. Over time, legally adopted children have become synonymous with biological children in the law. However, inheritance involving children who have become part of a family through in-vitro fertilization, adoption from a foreign country, or remarriage of one or both parents following divorce can become tricky.

A child born outside a legally recognized union — in most states, this is defined as a marriage between a woman and a man, but it is changing — will automatically inherit the mother's estate. An inheritance from the biological father is not automatic. This has been the case in California.

Many states, including California, will allow a child to inherit from a man who is identified as the father through a paternity test. The father can also marry the mother after the child is born and acknowledge himself as the father. If action is not taken to establish the biological relationship of an adult to a child, a child cannot inherit from the estate of the unidentified parent.

A parent can disinherit a child by express provisions of a will. But silence on the existence of a child in a will might raise the question of the testator's intent to disinherit, and the child might prevail in taking a share of the estate anyway.

☑ Watch Out for This

- ☐ You must legally adopt stepchildren for them to be considered part of your family; if you do not adopt them, and your will directs your estate to establish trust funds for your "children," only those minors who are recognized by the state as yours will be able to receive a bequest.

- ☐ A paternity test is the comparison of blood taken from the potential father against a blood sample of the child.

- ☐ A paternity suit is a legal action that is initiated to establish a man as the biological father of a child.

☐ While the question of paternity is typically associated with the father, a genetic test can be used to establish the biological relationship of a mother in the case of abandonment or other circumstances in which a mother is not clearly identified.

Nuncupative will: Also called an oral will, this is a spoken will. Some states only allow this kind of will if someone is literally on his or her deathbed, and it only covers personal property of little or no value. California has an oral will statute that prescribes certain conditions be met. *This is discussed further in Chapter 11.*

Video will: In most cases, a will recorded on a videotape or DVD will not be accepted as a legal document. Some states will, in extreme circumstances, allow a terminally ill person to literally record a will from a deathbed. Recording messages for loved ones might be something you want to do, but it is better to prepare legal documents, such as a will, with a lawyer. California does not recognize video wills unless they are accompanied by a written will.

It is important to consider how the will you prepare will complement or conflict with other elements of your estate plan.

The "Other" Will

Many people prepare a living will at the time they draw up the will for their estate even though it has nothing to do with your house, car, or checking account. A living will or medical directive is a document in which you spell out the decisions you have made about your medical care while you are still alive. The idea is to decide which kind of measures you want — or do not want — taken on your behalf if you should become incapacitated.

• *Did You Know?* •

The Health Insurance Portability and Accountability Act (HIPAA) is a federal law passed in 1996 that did more than just create additional forms for you to sign when you go to the doctor's office. It protects medical insurance coverage for employees when they change or lose their jobs. It also forced the creation and implementation of national standards for conducting electronic medical care transactions for providers, insurance companies and plans, and employers. But it also put into place privacy protections that prevent caregivers from sharing your personal information with anyone you did not explicitly authorize.

Questions were raised about the access to private information for someone holding a health care or medical power of attorney: Can medical staff give that person confidential medical information to make informed decisions as the incapacitated person expected?

The answer is yes. A form explicitly giving your designated person access to your information is not necessary. The U.S. Department of Health and Human Services confirmed the power of attorney supersedes the HIPAA privacy requirements.

It is still a good idea to make sure all your medical care providers, including primary care physician, eye doctor, dentist, and any specialists, have a copy of your health care or medical power of attorney on file. This can help avoid delays in case of an emergency.

All states, including California, now recognize living wills, but the documents are not uniform. Some states will only allow living wills to apply to a person who is permanently unconscious or has a terminal illness. Others will allow them for illnesses in advanced stages, such as the final stages of Alzheimer's, when death is not imminent.

To make sure your wishes are followed, you need to understand what California law does and does not allow. A statutory living will is one that complies with the statutes, or laws, of your state. In California, this option is more powerful than a living will. It is an Advanced Health Care Directive. *This is discussed further in Chapter 11.*

A nonstatutory living will does not comply with the laws of California. The differences between a statutory and nonstatutory living will might seem obvious, but like most legalities, the details are critical. A statutory document will likely provide more protection for the physicians and nurses carrying out your wishes.

Wording is also essential. A statement such as, "I do not want to become a burden to my family" is vague. Your living will should be specific and address your medical history, so consulting your doctor about potential scenarios is essential to understanding which kinds of lifesaving measures might be taken to keep you alive. If you have a history of congestive heart failure in your family and have been diagnosed with the same condition but do not want extraordinary measures, such as a feeding tube or respirator, taken to prolong your life, your wish needs to be spelled out.

Another way to make sure your wishes are followed regarding your medical care is to designate a health care power of attorney (HCPA), also known as a medical power of attorney. Your HCPA involves signing a legal document known as a power of attorney to designate a person to make medical decisions for you when you cannot do it for yourself. Many states have laws that allow family members to make some or all of your health care decisions. These family consent or health surrogate laws follow a specific order of kinship for who makes a decision; if you are married, your spouse will be your surrogate. Even though the default position of most physicians is to consult the family, having your wishes spelled out in an HCPA relieves your family of having to deal with that issue.

A durable power of attorney can also be used to give someone else the authority to make medical decisions on your behalf. This kind of power of attorney allows an authorized person to act on behalf of the grantor of that power of attorney.

Making decisions about life-sustaining treatment, artificial nutrition and hydration, and organ donation are the advanced directives most people prepare. A DNR order is an example of the kind of decision you can make and communicate in your living will. Completing an organ donor card will reinforce your decision to make that gift if it is important to you.

To avoid confusion or conflict at a later date, make sure your living will is properly executed with witnesses present. Then, make sure close family members and friends have copies of the document and understand your wishes. When a medical decision needs to be made, there is not any question about what you would want.

People Speaking for You

After you are no longer able to speak for yourself, others will speak on your behalf. Those individuals you choose to act for you have a host of legal and moral issues to manage, so choosing who will represent you is a serious matter. The lawyer preparing your will and the executor of your will are the two people who will have the most immediate and significant impact on what happens after you are gone. To choose the best people for these tasks, it is important to know what they do.

Wills attorney

The lawyer you retain to draw up your will should be experienced in probate and estate planning. In addition to being well-versed in federal law regarding estates, he or she also needs to know what California requires for a will to be valid and legal. If your estate planning process includes several planning professionals, such as a CPA or financial planner, your lawyer also should be someone who works well with others.

The more elusive criteria for choosing your legal representative are those that give you a sense you can trust and work with this person. You need to be able to share all the details of your life that will go into the composition of your estate. Your wishes for the devise of your property are intensely personal, and you must be able to be complete and candid with your attorney so he or she will be able to give you the best advice. You also need to be comfortable going back repeatedly to make changes to your will and estate plan so you keep up with changes in your life and, sometimes, the law.

It is also important you are able to communicate comfortably and effectively with the person who will manage your estate.

Executor

After you are gone, you want someone to take care of your estate the way you would. That means finding the right person or company to handle the steps that need to be taken after you die. Regardless of the individual(s) you select, this person must do the following things:

- Guide your will through the probate process to make sure it is accepted as valid. This also means defending the will against any contest challenges.

- Collect your assets.

- Oversee the transition of gifts made to beneficiaries. This might include a title transfer for a house or making sure a life insurance policy check is made out in the correct name.

- Review, evaluate, and pay any claims against your estate. These include taxes and outstanding bills that are owed.

- Raise the money to pay claims. This can mean selling assets, such as a house or car.

- Prepare and file an accounting of all financial transactions for the court.

Failure to do any of these things can have serious consequences for the executor, so it is extremely important the person who agrees to take on this responsibility knows what is expected.

Because this is such a time-consuming, key responsibility, you do have the option to pay your executor a fee for his or her services. Whether you should do this is a decision to discuss with your lawyer.

Although predicting how someone will handle this kind of responsibility is impossible, giving careful thought to who will carry out your wishes is important.

Change and Your Will

Simply put, things happen. That is why it is essential to make sure changes you experience in your life are reflected in your will. Once a will is written, it is not etched in stone. It can be revised or even replaced.

To make a change to a specific portion of your will, create a codicil. This is a separate legal document that adds to your existing will. It is an easy way to make a few simple changes. When you are older, a codicil is an easy way to protect your will from being challenged due to incompetence. If you only change one part, the codicil might be successfully challenged but not the majority of your will.

You might change your will without even realizing it. If you bequest specific property to someone, such as a boat, then you sell it or it sinks during a storm, it will be addressed by the court. No matter what the reason, if property is missing from your estate that is named in your will, it is considered adeemed. Ademption statutes govern the distribution of your belongings, and the state will take over if items are missing. There are ways to avoid this problem, such as having backup property to serve as a substitute or other provision you wish to make.

If a beneficiary in your will dies before you do, the gift in the will to the beneficiary is said to have lapsed. Some states, like California, have an anti-lapse statute to cover how the lapsed gift should be distributed and prevent arguments. California has an anti-lapse statute that provides the following alternatives: If the will provides an alternative beneficiary, that is the resolution; if the will is silent and the beneficiary is not related to the testator, the gift becomes part of the residue of the estate and goes to the beneficiary of the residuary clause of the will; if the intended beneficiary was a blood relative of the testator or the testator's spouse, the gift will be distributed to the beneficiary's lawful descendant(s).

Another similar type of situation can arise called ademption in which the testator already gave the beneficiary the bequest named in the will before dying. An example is Aunt Mary's antique silver collection bequeathed to niece Jane. In California, the bequest is satisfied as to Jane — or adeemed — only if the will specifically mentions Jane already has it or Jane agrees in writing the gift was given her in satisfaction of the will's bequest and it is the exact same set of antique silver. Otherwise, Jane might be entitled to an equivalent value of the bequest from the estate because there was no intent to adeem the gift before Aunty Mary died.

Note that both ademption and abatement issues are avoidable by express provisions in the will covering how the testator wishes potential circumstances to be handled.

Maybe at the time of your death, you are carrying a ton of debt that you were going to pay off in the near future. An unexpected departure is something you can plan for in your will. The usual method for paying off debt is to sell property in the estate, such as jewelry, antiques, or vacation property. But if there still is not enough money to take care of those debts, your house might have to be sold, which would leave your family homeless. Some states have a homestead exemption statute that protects the family home from being sold or at least up to a dollar value of the home. California has an automatic homestead exemption of up to $75,000. This amount increases to $100,000 if a member of the immediate family, such as a minor child, is living in the house and has no ownership interest in it. For people who are disabled or older than 65, the exemption increases to $175,000. Many other states are less protective. To understand how the exemption works, it is best to get advice from your estate-planning team.

CHAPTER 6

Trusts

The image many people have of a child with a trust fund is someone with access to all the money necessary to pay for a college education and an extended tour of Europe or have a carefree future without money problems. The truth is you do not have to be independently wealthy to set up a trust, and their uses are significantly more diverse than these stereotypes.

The basic idea behind a trust is to set aside specific property for specific people or institutions so you, not the courts, decide what will happen to your estate. Knowing what you want to put into the trust; who benefits from the trust; and what the costs are, such as set-up fees, taxes, and time, is essential to making sure you choose the right trust.

There are at least a dozen different kinds of trusts with various combinations of legal and tax implications, so there is no such thing as a "standard" trust. This book can help you learn what a trust is, but any standardized trust template is a disaster waiting to happen.

Each trust is customized to meet the needs of the individual. That is what makes a trust so attractive and difficult. Laws and tax requirements at the federal and state level are constantly changing, and so are your needs. With the possibility that your trust could end up in probate or in the hands of the government, it is essential to work with an estate planner and lawyer to make sure you have the proper documents in place so your trust is legal and enforceable.

To make sure the outcome you want is the one you get, learn what a trust is and its benefits and drawbacks. The steps to set up a trust and the elements of a trust can be easy enough to understand: Identify which property will be included, who benefits, who manages the trust, what the tax implications are for all the people involved, and how the law governs all that activity. The tricky part is learning about the different kinds of trusts and matching them up with your wishes.

What is a Trust?

A trust is a legal arrangement that transfers property from the original owner to a person or a company for the purpose of holding and maintaining the property until it is handed over to the beneficiary, the individual or institution designated to receive the property.

It seems straightforward until you get into the many legal terms, people, laws, and taxes that go into the creation of a trust. With many interchangeable terms, some of which are as confusing as the Greek or Roman terms from which they originated, a list of who is who and what is what is helpful. The following situation will help you recognize the roles each person plays in a trust.

Scenario: Aunt Tara wants to set up a trust for her house so her niece Betsy will have a place to set up her veterinary clinic after she finishes her education. But she does not know when Betsy will graduate, so she wants her grandson Charles to take care of the place if she dies. In case something happens to Charles, his wife, Kim, will take on that responsibility.

- **Trustor (Aunt Tara):** The person who sets up the trust. Other names commonly used are creator, donor, settlor, or grantor.

- **Beneficiary (Betsy):** The individual(s) or group(s) that will receive the property in the trust. This can be a single person, multiple people, one group, several groups, or a combination of any of these.

- **Trustee (Charles):** The person or company that will oversee or manage the trust once it is established. This person or group will make sure the property in the trust is safe and in good order until it is turned over to the beneficiary. This includes paying taxes, performing repairs, and doing anything else an owner would do. The trustee is obligated to carry out the terms of the trust and can be paid for this effort if terms for this are included in the trust language.

- **Successor trustee (Kim):** Someone who will step in if the primary trustee is unable to serve or cannot continue to manage your trust. This person will have the same legal obligations for managing the trust as the original trustee if he or she assumes the management responsibilities.

The individual or company designated to serve as trustee carries a significant amount of responsibility and should be someone you trust. Consider the potential for conflict of interest or the temptation to do something inappropriate, such as stealing from the trust or neglecting the work. Putting language in the trust documents that spells out the responsibilities of the trustees is essential, and creating a mechanism of oversight and removal will also prevent your heirs from losing what is supposed to be theirs.

Things and strings: Aunt Tara's house sits on 4 acres of land with an outbuilding to store the lawn tractor and other equipment. Over the years, she sold the other 12 acres, so she invested the money in a mutual fund. Aunt Tara had her lawyer set up a trust fund that gives Betsy the interest from the mutual fund to pay tuition when it is due in the fall, but Aunt Tara's mutual fund will not go to Betsy until she graduates from college. The house in the care of Charles will also go to Betsy after she graduates.

- **Property:** Also referred to as principal, anything you want to give to other people. There are all kinds of legal terms for what you own, and you have to make sure you use the right words to identify everything: money in a safe, a checking account, a rocking chair or a commemorative baseball. Property can be real property or real estate, such as a 10-acre farm; tangible personal property you can touch, such as a lawn tractor and other equipment; or intangible personal property, such as financial assets.

- **Trust agreement:** The legal document that spells out the terms of a trust, including the people and conditions and the rules that must be followed. Some are state or federal laws and others are specific conditions, such as a trust fund.

- **Funding a trust:** The placement of property in a trust; that same property will be called trust principal once it is under the auspices of the trust agreement.

- **Provisions:** The clauses that spell out how you want your wishes carried out. Distribution provisions will identify to whom the income will be given and how often it will be distributed, for example every fall when tuition bills are due. Special provisions encompass all requirements that are specific to the beneficiary or the assets, for example graduation from college.

- **Legal title:** This gives the trustee ownership of the property in the trust for the duration of the trustee's responsibility, for example putting the house in Charles' care.

- **Beneficial title:** Also known as equitable title, this is the right of the person or institution to take possession of or benefit from the property in the trust, for example when Betsy receives the property.

The plan can be clear, but whether the end result matches that plan depends on the kind of trust you choose, the way the documents are worded, and the way the people involved carry out their tasks. It is easier to make mistakes than it is to get it right, and those mistakes can be costly for loved ones. If you are not careful, they can inherit a big mess instead of the things you want them to have.

One way to avoid such a mess is to carefully choose a trustee who will carry out your wishes and do so legally. Being a trustee is more than just whipping out a checkbook and signing a few papers now and then.

Talking to Your Estate Planner About Trusts

Before you sit down with your estate planner, think abo[ut the ques]tions you have regarding your life circumstances. Here are a few:

- What are the tax consequences for this trust? What about capital gains?

- What happens to the leftovers in a trust: cash, property, and everything else?

- Will there be a problem if the trust beneficiary dies before you do?

- What happens if the terms of a trust are not met? For example, Bobby quits school before spending his educational trust.

- When does a specific use trust terminate? For example, Aunt Mimi's disability trust is still in place after she dies.

- What happens to an irrevocable trust if the situation changes?

- What are the advantages and disadvantages for a single person in setting up a trust?

- What happens if some of the property in your trust is community property and you divorce?

- If you end up divorced, what happens to the education trust fund that Mom and Dad are funding for Suzy?

Things to consider...

An estate planner can also help you address some of the unexpected or unusual life circumstances that might not be on your mind. There are also legal ramifications that might not come up while you're alive. For example, unmarried partners do not get the same automatic consideration that a legally married couple has. A qualified terminable interest property trust (QTIP) is not an option for a couple who does not have a legally documented marriage.

Some other things that affect the legality and terms of a trust include:

- Foreign-born spouse

- Nonbiological family members

- Same-sex couples

- Living together without a formal or common-law marriage

- Adoption

- Pets

- Divorce

- The children and spouses from multiple marriages

- Incapacitation

- Medical conditions and serious illness

- Permanent disability

- Property damaged by natural disaster

- Stock and real estate market crashes

Types of Trusts

A trust can be set up to take effect while you are alive, which is inter vivos, or it can take effect after you die, which is testamentary. Some are revocable, or can be changed, and some are irrevocable, or cannot be changed. Some trusts can be terminated or ended while others cannot. Depending on what the current tax law allows, the purpose of a trust can result in a tax exemption or a higher tax rate.

Many of the reasons for setting up a trust for yourself or for other people are the same: getting tax benefits, staying out of probate court, protecting assets from creditors, or making sure money is available for education, severe illness, a disability, or other matters. Deciding which trust would be most helpful by considering all the possibilities in life is a daunting task. Another way to look at the situation is to consider the kinds of trusts that already exist and have defined legal and tax consequences.

Trusts fall into a number of categories based on different criteria. One criterion is the beneficiary. A marital-dedicational trust is specific to the surviving, legal spouse of the deceased. A bypass trust will transfer property to someone other than your spouse, such as a child or grandchild, but allow him to still benefit from the property in the trust. Many states even allow you to create a trust for your pets. California enacted a 2008 law that allows the creation of pet trusts for domestic animals. Previously, such trusts were not recognized as legal instruments. The animal owner can designate a trustee and sum of money for the trust to care for the animal during its lifetime after the owner dies or if the owner becomes incapacitated. A trustee can be subject to court review if an animal welfare agency or an heir of the owner challenges how the money is being used for the animal or whether the sum for the animal's care seems excessive. A pet trust is not considered a charitable trust; however, arrangements could be made for the animal's care through a nonprofit agency.

As the pet trust concept suggests, another criterion for how you set up a trust is the reason for the trust. If you wanted to protect the beneficiary's property so it is available for a specific reason when he or she needs it, you would use a protective trust. A discretionary trust gives the trustee the ability to distribute income and property to a variety of beneficiaries; he or she also has the option to control the distributions to a single beneficiary as he or she decides is appropriate. That offers some flexibility, and so does a dynasty trust. Also known as a wealth trust, it can last for several generations, or be set up to never end. This kind of trust helps people with a vast amount of wealth control the distribution of that money and property over a long period of time. However, many states, including California, limit noncharitable trusts to 90 years.

The overarching requirements of a trust create another group. A split-interest means more than one individual benefits from the trust. One person or charity would have an interest in the trust for a specific period of time, and then another person or charity receives the property that remains. A support trust requires a trustee to pay only the income and property necessary to cover the cost of education of or assistance, such as health care or nursing home fees, for the beneficiaries.

Some trusts are automatically irrevocable, so you have to make sure you know what you are signing before you pick up the pen. However, many trusts can be set up as revocable or irrevocable with a variety of conditions that put the trust into one of the categories tax law already defines. These laws change to keep up with people's creative efforts to avoid taxes.

These conditions and restrictions make it important to consult an estate-planning specialist. Discuss the trust options that will help you achieve your goals, and understand the tax implications of your choices.

The following is a list of the different types of trusts:

- **Burial trust:** Provides the funds necessary to cover the cost of your burial or cremation arrangements. This can be a revocable trust, but after your death, it becomes irrevocable, and the trust cannot be used for anything else.

- **Charitable trust:** Offers the benefits of tax-free gifts for the donor. A charitable remainder trust gives gifts of interest income that are paid to specific beneficiaries, such as your spouse, for a specific period of time. At the end of that time period, a charity receives whatever is left in the trust. A charitable lead trust, or a front trust, gives the charity a specific gift before all other beneficiaries receive anything. These are both split-interest trusts. Split-interest trusts make distributions to both charitable and noncharitable beneficiaries while providing tax benefits to their donor.

- **Crummey trust:** This is an exceedingly complicated trust normally set up in conjunction with an irrevocable life insurance trust to make the payments for a life insurance policy. This kind of trust requires an estate-planning attorney.

- **Educational trust:** This is a kind of protective trust that sets aside money specifically for education-related expenses, such as tuition or training fees, books, or supplies. These trusts regularly include provisions to stop payments if the student drops out of school or flunks many classes.

- **Generation-skipping transfer trust (GSTT):** A tax-saving trust designed to benefit multiple generations after you are gone.

- **Grantor-retained trusts:** These are irrevocable and noncharitable, which means they cannot be changed and the beneficiary is not a charity. There are three common types: A grantor-retained annuity trust (GRAT) gives a fixed amount of money at predetermined, often regularly scheduled, times; a grantor-retained unit trust (GRUT) pays a specific percentage to the beneficiary; and a grantor-retained incomes trust (GRIT) designates specific people to receive certain property, such as stocks or a house, but the income or use of the property stays with you until your death.

- **Living trust:** Created while you are still alive, this trust allows you to be the grantor, trustee, and beneficiary, if you choose.

- **Marital dedication trust:** Property goes into a trust that is exclusively for your spouse, who decides what happens to the property after your death.

- **Minor trust:** This is a way to give gifts to minors that avoids the gift tax and keeps the property safe until the minor becomes an adult and can take ownership of the trust.

- **QTIP:** A qualified terminable interest property trust is a marital deduction trust. But instead of your spouse deciding who gets the property after your death, the grantor makes that decision.

- **Spendthrift trust:** A trust that is set up for someone who will not be able to handle their own affairs because, for example, he or she is mentally incompetent or has financial problems and needs protection from creditors. The beneficiary owns the payments made from the trust but not the property in the trust.

- **Special needs trust:** A support trust for a disabled person, including yourself, under the age of 65, this trust makes payments on the beneficiary's behalf as required by the state as reimbursement. After the beneficiary dies, the property in the trust is paid to other beneficiaries. This trust is designed to protect your property from government seizure or from a creditor seeking reimbursement.

- **Supplemental needs trust:** This support trust is designed to provide income to a handicapped, elderly, or disabled person to supplement their income, but it is structured in a way that does not reduce or jeopardize the eligibility of that person to receive public or private benefits. This trust is designed to protect your property from government seizure or from a creditor seeking reimbursement.

- **Testamentary trust:** The terms of your will create this trust after your death.

- **Totten trust:** This is a bank account that, upon your death, immediately passes to the named beneficiary.

There are also special trusts for specific things, such as real estate, life insurance, or pension benefits. Choosing which trust will meet your needs and those of your estate is a difficult process. This information can help you familiarize yourself with the choices that are out there, but an estate-planning specialist is the best person to help you decide whether you need a trust and which one will be the best choice.

• *Did You Know?* •

If you have a modest estate but you still want your minor children to inherit your property, you can use the Uniform Transfer for Minors Act (UTMA) or the Uniform Gift to Minors Act (UGMA). Most states, including California, have adopted the UTMA, which allows you to create a custodian account for a minor.

A custodian account, which can be in the form of a trust, allows you to deposit money or property in an account set up by a bank or a brokerage firm. You name yourself as the custodian, or trustee, of the account while you are alive and name a successor to take over those responsibilities after you die. This new custodian will serve in that capacity until the child reaches 18, 21, or 25, depending on the state law. It is 18 in California.

☑ Watch Out for This

- ☐ Some states hand over the ownership of the account to the child when he or she turns 18, and you have no say after that.

- ☐ Accounts for children over the age of 13 are subject to federal income tax at the children's rate. This will most certainly be lower than your tax rate, but consider the implications of this.

- ☐ If you create an UGMA or UTMA account, this can reduce the amount of court paperwork and supervision, which lowers estate costs.

- ☐ Even if you create this kind of account, you must still name a legal guardian for your children in your will. The legal guardian can also be custodian of this kind of account, but naming a custodian of an account is not the same as naming a legal guardian.

Pros and Cons of Forming a Trust

Trusts provide some excellent benefits, but they are not the perfect solution for everything. One benefit is some trusts can reduce the amount of taxes that have to be paid before and after you die. However, if your trust is not set up properly, you might have to pay income tax. A trust can protect your or your beneficiaries' assets from your creditors only if it is set up properly.

More private than a will, which becomes public record upon your death and makes the details of your estate available to anyone who wants access, a trust can keep others out of your personal business. In many cases, a trust can help keep your estate out of probate court, and it is more difficult to contest a trust than a will. The flexibility of a trust allows you to make changes and can even help with financial issues if you become disabled during your life.

The downside is that it costs money to set up a trust, and there are numerous foreign and domestic scams out there. If you are not careful, you could lose the property you want to go to your loved ones and charity. That your trustee will abscond with the contents of the trusts and head for a country that will not extradite him or her is also a possibility.

Whether trusts are worth all the hassle and potential risk is up to you, and that is why is it essential to work with estate-planning specialists when setting up any trust(s).

Dos and Don'ts for Trusts

Consider the following tips when you are preparing your trust:

- Think of choosing a trust as a dry run for your estate planning. Consider all possible life scenarios and the way a trust would help those situations.

- When setting up a trust or trusts, do them all at once so, with any luck, you can save a few dollars and make sure none of them conflict with the others.

- Put all trust agreements in writing.

- Make sure to use the proper legal language in every agreement.

- Clearly define the trustee responsibilities and obligations. The court might not recognize a passive trust, which does not define these things, as a trust.

- Clearly identify beneficiaries.

- Clearly define the property in the trust. Don't just say, "Everything in the dining room."

- Make sure the property you put into a trust will meet the needs you identify. Setting $100,000 aside to pay for a college education might not be enough in 2100.

- Carefully choose a trustee who will execute your wishes, take care of all legal obligations, and be willing to take on all those duties.

- Keep an eye on the content and value of each trust over time. Fluctuating market conditions and changes in your life might leave a trust underfunded, or it might become obsolete.

Notes about other information you want to learn:

_____

_____

_____

_____

_____

CHAPTER 7

Insurance

Insurance is one part of your estate plan, and it can be an especially effective part if you have good information. Get advice tailored to your needs, not advice of the person pushing papers across the desk for you to sign. How you want to make that money work for you should guide your shopping and decision making. Consider:

- **Funeral expenses:** On average, these range from $5,000 to $8,000 but can go much higher.

- **Grief money:** Support your family during their grieving period so they do not have to rush back to work to cover the bills.

- **Debts:** Cover what you owe to others so it does not reduce the size of your estate.

- **Estate costs:** Ready cash to cover estate taxes and estate distribution costs, and provide a stipend for your executor.

- **Lost income:** Give your family access to some of the income you would have earned.

- **Education funds:** Provide money for school now or in the future.

- **Funding a trust:** This will add to the property in the trust and be distributed like all the other assets in that trust.

- **Taxes:** Make sure your estate has enough money to cover tax payment to state and federal tax collectors.

For a small investment, you can provide your beneficiaries with a substantial amount of money if you choose carefully.

When you die, the insurance company that holds your life insurance policy cuts a check to your spouse, children, or parents, but there is much more to know, including the following:

- Death benefits can be taxed.

- If the beneficiary of your policy dies before you do, the money goes into probate.

- An insurance policy that invests in the stock market might actually lose value and leave your beneficiaries with less money.

- A serious illness can devastate the assets of your estate, which means the life insurance you wanted to support your family could end up in the hands of creditors instead.

Insurance is not quite as simple as it once was or as sales reps like to make it appear. The kind of insurance you have when you are alive can affect your estate as much as the insurance you have for after your death, so this is where the here and now affects the future.

Simply defined, insurance, is a method to protect the things we value most. Some insurance is mandated by law, such as automobile insurance; some is considered essential, such as home insurance; and other kinds are considered a luxury, such disability and long-term care. What kind and how much insurance any individual needs are based on his or her circumstances. If you do not have a $20 million country estate, it is not likely you are going to need the kind of liability insurance that would protect you against a lawsuit brought by someone who stayed for the weekend and was hurt while riding a horse from your stable.

As part of your overall estate plan, insurance can accomplish some of the more conventional goals people have, such as providing cash to pay taxes so your family does not have to sell property to settle with the government. What is slightly more uncommon is considering the impact a permanent disability can have on the assets of your estate and how you will maintain that estate until it is passed on to someone else.

Thinking about insurance before you need it is the best way to consider the host of options and tangle of details and conditions related to each. This requires speculation on your part, but educated guesses are possible when you make time to let your imagination run free.

Insurance for Here and Now

Most insurance commercials focus on the worst-case scenario to scare you into buying peace of mind. Though horrible, these situations are exactly what you need to consider. Considering the effects of a serious illness, debilitating accident, or natural disaster can point you in the right directions for figuring out your insurance needs.

Medical insurance

Frequently referred to as health insurance by those who sell it, the insurance that covers medical costs is almost never used when you are healthy. But you always have to whip out that benefits card when you fill a prescription for strep throat, have a heart attack, or break a bone.

The first question you need to consider is whether your insurance policy will cover your bills when you truly need it to. If your insurance does not pay, you will have to. That payment can be high enough to wipe out your savings and any other assets you have built up over time. What most people consider is the amount that is deducted from every paycheck week after week, not the tens of thousands of dollars a hospital will try to collect from you after you have hit your maximum lifetime benefit.

Even if your family has no history of colon cancer, breast cancer, heart attack, or even high cholesterol, you could still be involved in a workplace accident or a horrible car crash that is not your fault or contract a rare virus on the only trip you ever take out of the country. Anyone who has children or knows someone who has children knows that trips to the emergency room and doctor's office are the rule, not the exception.

A simple cold going around school can land your child in an intensive care unit with walking pneumonia. Will your insurance cover a stay in a pediatric ICU? What if your child requires hospitalization while out of state visiting relatives? Knowing the terms of your medical insurance coverage, beyond the monthly premium, is an essential part of your estate planning. A few simple things to check are:

- What is the maximum lifetime benefit per person? Per policy?

- Which serious illnesses are not covered?

- How is a pre-existing condition defined, and can that be excluded from your coverage?

- Do you have out-of-network coverage? Can you purchase additional coverage if you are going to travel out of your network area? Out of the country?

- Can you get reimbursed for medical care provided outside the United States?

- When can you make changes to your coverage?

After you find the answers to these questions, compare the information against your family medical history. Do any of the illnesses not covered run in your family? Also, consider what is on the horizon for your family, such as a child going to study abroad for a year or an overweight spouse starting a new exercise program without consulting a doctor. Paying a slightly higher premium now for better coverage can prevent some devastating bills later.

A person who receives a diagnosis of cancer typically does not begin thinking about funding a family trip to Bermuda. He is thinking about receiving extensive treatment, not being able to coach Little League, and maybe missing work for an extended period of time. Do not leave everything in the hands of your insurance agent. Preparing for these situations is your job.

Disability insurance

A disability insurance policy will make payments to cover living expenses and replace your lost income as a result of your inability to hold a job. If you cannot work because you are sick or get hurt or for some other reason, this insurance will replace some of your lost income. Imagine what could happen to your savings if you are stuck at home in bed but the mortgage payment, utility bills, and furnace repair invoices keep coming.

Your ability to leave anything for your loved ones after you are gone depends on the work you do while you are alive. Though disability insurance will not replace 100 percent of your income, it would certainly be better than nothing. The question is whether the conditions and restrictions make it a worthwhile investment for you. If you feel it is a good idea, determine which kind of disability insurance will meet your needs.

Many different disability plans are out there, but they fall into two types: short- or long-term. Short-term disability provides benefits for about three months. Some plans go a little longer, but they are a temporary fix. Long-term disability can provide benefits for years but eventually ends, frequently at 65, when you become eligible for Social Security. The benefits are as varied as the plans available. Some details to look for include:

- ***When the policy goes into effect:*** Some policies do not begin to make payments until you have been out of work for a specific period of time. They do not make payments the moment you are disabled.

- ***How payments are calculated:*** Some policies replace, on average, between 50 and 75 percent of your income.

- ***Definition of disability:*** You might have to be unable to work at any job to receive payments, or they might be made if you are not able to work in your chosen profession.

- ***Premium payments:*** How they are calculated can depend on the percentage of income replaced, for example more money means a higher premium, or some other criterion.

The federal government also provides a Social Security disability benefit for which you might be eligible. But do not count on the government to reimburse 100 percent of your income. If you think only 50 percent of your income reimbursed is not enough, consider other options.

Although short-term disability can help you through a rough time, long-term disability is going to have a direct impact on your estate plan. A serious injury not only has the potential to rack up major medical bills health insurance does not cover, but the costs can also eliminate the possibility of future investments and jeopardize your ability to pay life insurance and other premiums.

Long-term care insurance

The difference between long-term disability and long-term care insurance is the latter provides payments to cover the cost of medical care. In-home nursing or nursing home fees are examples of what might be covered. Although you might think this is only for 89-year-old Aunt Mary who could fall and break her hip, but this coverage is for any debilitating injury suffered by anyone at any age.

If you fall at work and injure your back so badly you require surgery and months of physical therapy to walk again, your medical insurance might not be enough to cover the entire cost. Understand what your policy will and will not cover and when the payments will begin. If you max out your medical insurance, but your long-term care insurance does not kick in for a year, if ever, the assets in your estate could be in jeopardy.

Looking into all these details before you need to use your insurance is the best way to learn what you need to know. Do not leave it to your family to sort out.

Homeowner's and renter's insurance

If your house is your biggest asset, protecting it is a no-brainer. The list of possible disasters can keep homeowners up all night immediately before and after buying a house. A down payment and an hour's worth of signing papers will make you realize what is on the line if something goes wrong. Banks do not forgive your loan because your house burns down.

Even if you do not own a home, that lease you signed is a legally binding agreement. If you are robbed or the pipes in the apartment above add a waterfall feature to your living room, you are still going to have to pay your rent, and the antique books you wanted to give to your niece Amy will not be worth anything wet.

Making sure you can recover the loss of your property, both real estate and personal belongings, is essential if your estate is to have any value after a disaster, natural or otherwise. Consider fire, flood, earthquakes, tornadoes, heavy snow, heavy wind, and anything else that might damage your home and its contents when purchasing insurance.

Some homeowners' policies will pay off the balance of a home mortgage and leave the bulk of your estate to replace your income if you do not want your family to worry about money after you are gone. Before signing on that dotted line, find out the circumstances under which the policy might not pay off the mortgage. Just because you die does not mean they will pay up.

Automobile insurance

An antique or exotic car collection would warrant an automobile insurance policy with special coverage for the replacement of such a rare vehicle, but the average driver will need a policy that covers the basics.

If you lease a car, you know the leasing agency requires specific limits for personal injury and liability. California also requires a minimum amount of insurance coverage to legally drive your car. If you have no insurance, you can have your driver's license suspended or revoked. None of this is likely to be a surprise; what might become a surprise is what happens if you are sued or agree to a settlement after an automobile accident and you do not have insurance.

If you have teenagers starting to drive, you know your premiums are going to go up. Car rental agencies figured out the risk of young drivers a long time ago and require a driver to be 25 to sign a rental agreement. Be prepared for this when you have to add another driver to your policy. Also check the per-accident and per-person payout amounts because they make a difference.

Car insurance only pays out to the limits in your policy. If you want a cheap premium and do not bother to look at what those payouts are, you could end up having to pay a considerable sum. Getting their hands on hundreds of thousands of dollars is not easy for most people, so part of your estate planning is checking into your automobile coverage and deciding whether it is adequate.

Umbrella liability insurance

This kind of policy adds property protection that goes beyond homeowner's, renter's, automobile, or any other kind of insurance. If the person you rear-end at a red light thinks you have a good amount of money, he might sue you for that reason. It is not fair you should have to defend yourself against a frivolous lawsuit, but it is better not to lose your house or other property because you did not have adequate protection.

When looking into this kind of insurance, it is important to know what is and is not covered. Look for loopholes that will allow the insurance company to wiggle out of paying a claim.

An umbrella policy is not going to be necessary for everyone, but it is often essential for people with a valuable estate because they have plenty to lose before they have a chance to pass it on. Cross of your list an insurance agent who tells you anything to the contrary.

Shopping for an insurance agent you can trust is going to take some time, but the benefits are valuable. Only if you do your homework will you make sense of all the possible options, understand the fine print of all those options, and know the legalities of making changes and still having your beneficiaries receive what you expect them to.

Details, Details

Insurance is all about the details, so be sure to ask plenty of questions and become extremely clear about what can, might, should, and will not happen related to your policies. Ask the hard questions, and do not accept anything less than a full response:

- Under which circumstances will the benefit not be paid? Find out all degrees of risk, including the worst-case scenario.

- Which of my assets are at risk, and from what?

- Which kinds of safety nets can insurance provide?

- Considering the details of my estate, which kind of insurance does not have a good balance between cost and benefit?

- What amount of coverage is excessive for my situation?

- What are the varying degrees of risk among my possible choices, if any?

- Why would my estate planning team reject your recommendation?

Policies

With so many options, selecting what you need can be difficult. Check off those you think you might like to include in your estate plan, and then work with an agent to determine whether you need this kind of coverage.

While you are alive:

_____ Medical

_____ Dental

_____ Vision

_____ Long-term disability

_____ Short-term disability

_____ Long-term care

_____ Homeowner's or renter's

_____ Car

_____ Umbrella liability

After death:

_____ Life

_____ Whole life

_____ Universal life

_____ Joint first-to-die or second-to-die

_____ Term life insurance

_____ Annual renewable

_____ Decreasing

_____ Level

_____ Group

_____ Funeral and burial

Insurance for After You Are Gone

Some insurance agents will tell you all you need is plenty of life insurance to make sure your loved ones are taken care of. But insurance is not that simple. As with wills and trusts, this protection theme has many variations. The following are different types of life insurance:

- **Whole life:** Sometimes called cash value life insurance, this is the kind of policy most people know. After qualifying based on certain criteria, such as whether you smoke, are a desk jockey or a bungee jumper, and are 25 or 75, qualified, the insured person pays a monthly premium. The policy will, upon his or her death, pay a predetermined, fixed amount of money to his or her beneficiaries. A portion of the fixed premium is invested and another portion is placed into an account, such as a savings account. That cash value is accessible to the policy owner. It can be borrowed against as a loan, or the cash can be taken as the proceeds of the policy instead of the death benefit payout.

o **Universal life:** A kind of whole life policy that guarantees a minimum return, but the value of the policy can go up or down. If the policy makes more money, the return might be high enough to cover your premium payments.

o **Joint first-to-die or second-to-die:** Just as it sounds, this is a policy two people hold, and the beneficiary is paid after the first person or second person dies. You decide the payout when you set the terms of the policy.

- **Term life insurance:** Carries an annual premium and pays a specified death benefit to the beneficiary, but it does not have a cash value, so you cannot borrow money from it. The only payment made is to the beneficiary. The premium is based on the amount of insurance you purchase, or what will be paid out after your death, and how old you are. Younger people pay less and, as they get older, their premiums rise accordingly. If you stop paying premiums, the death benefit is not paid. There are a number of different kinds of term policies available:

o **Annual renewable:** This has an annual premium and can be renewed from year to year. Be sure you understand the renewal rights before signing.

o **Decreasing:** Premiums remain the same, but the benefit decreases over time. For example, you purchase this kind of insurance, which is also known as mortgage or credit term insurance, to pay off your debts after you die. The mortgage you want to insure is $250,000 at the time you purchase the insurance, but the mortgage value when you die is $150,000; the policy pays $150,000. This kind of insurance is recommended only for those who cannot get any other kind of insurance.

o **Level:** Coverage is guaranteed for a specific period of time, or term, such as five, 10, or 20 years, at a specific premium. The premium will remain for the five-year period, but at year six, it will go up and remain at that rate through the 10th year and continue in that direction.

o **Group:** Employers frequently purchase a term life policy for each employee as an added benefit. Employees get an exceptionally low rate, and there is no income tax on the premiums for the first $50,000 of coverage.

• *Did You Know?* •

To receive the death benefit from a life insurance policy, a death certificate for the policy holder is required as proof of death.

The most expedient way for your executor to obtain a copy is through the mortuary or other institution that is responsible for handling the body of the deceased. Copies can also be obtained from the county health department.

☑ Watch Out for This

☐ Authorized copies of a death certificate are needed to provide proof of death. You cannot just reproduce a few dozen at your local copy center.

☐ Obtain several copies of the death certificate. Most institutions that require a certificate for proof will retain it for their files.

☐ Call the county health department to find out the current fee for the certificate.

Varying Beneficiaries

No matter which kind of insurance you decide to purchase, you can choose different beneficiaries. This depends on what the policy is going to do. To start, consider the goal of the policy and who will need or use that money for that purpose. A life insurance policy that is specifically set up to give your family time to grieve might name your spouse as the beneficiary because he or she, not your estate, will pay the utility bills and buy the groceries.

Regardless of whom you name as the beneficiary, it is important to name an alternative beneficiary. If the first beneficiary dies before you or declines the gift, the second person or institution you named will receive the benefit. If the death benefit goes unclaimed, it is added to your estate and heads to probate for distribution by the court. Depending on what is owed at the time of your death, creditors and others might get more of the money than family, friends, or a charity you wish to support.

Although there might be tax implications for insurance beneficiaries in certain circumstances, a lump sum life insurance policy payout is generally not taxable income. There can be exceptions. For example, interest accrued above the death benefit value that is included in the lump sum payout is generally taxable. If the beneficiary is your estate, whether by intention or default for lack of viable beneficiary at the time of your death, and the proceeds are paid into your probate estate, the proceeds become subject to estate or inheritance tax rules that might apply in your jurisdiction. When it comes to taxes on benefits, whether insurance or another form of gift, make no assumptions. Get the most current tax advice.

CASE STUDY: INSURANCE — MORE THAN LIFE COVERAGE

Linda Horn
Chief Executive Officer
Capital Concepts
linda@capitalconcepts.net
www.capitalconcepts.net

Some people only buy insurance, and others diversify their investments. What is the benefit of having a large amount of insurance?

Tax-free income to your family or a charity is a benefit. Proceeds from a policy often provide additional funds to pay the estate taxes. If you own a business or farm, insurance becomes critical to paying federal and state estate tax due within nine months of your death. Or perhaps you wish to leave a legacy for future generations or name a charity to continue your legacy.

What are the drawbacks of a large amount of insurance?

The premium payment should never create a financial hardship. After all, life is about living.

Consider under which circumstance an insurance company won't pay out a death benefit on various types of insurance, such as whole life, term life, or accidental death.

During the first two years after the issue date, the policy can be contested for suicide or false statements on the application about known medical history that can be attributed to your death. After two years, or if the above does not apply, all claims are paid.

How is disability insurance a valuable part of estate planning?

Disability is often overlooked when you have six times the probability of becoming disabled while on the job than of dying on the job. Your largest asset is your income. Protecting your income far exceeds your home, yet we would never consider having no homeowner's coverage.

Which other types of insurance beyond life are important to an estate plan?

Long-term care insurance is an essential part of your plan. Should you need long-term care, such as in a nursing home or assisted-living facility, your assets will quickly be diminished, and little will be left for your spouse or children. Waiting until you know you need it is like insuring your home when it is on fire; you cannot get it, and if you could, it would be expensive.

What are the benefits of working with an insurance professional?

If you are doing or have done your job of saving properly, a full-time professional is as necessary as the family doctor. A financial advisor works full-time for many years to gain the expertise to get you to your final destination with as few bumps in the road as possible. About 95 percent of do-it-your-selfers lose money while the revers is true for those who use a professional. The discipline of a balanced approach to risk management and investment will pay off. A good advisor will make you far more money than you ever pay them. Their access to information alone is worth the investment. You do not drill your own teeth or cut your own hair, so why would you invest your life savings with an amateur?

How does a person choose an insurance professional? Which characteristics and what experience should a potential client look for?

First, ask trusted friends for their recommendations. Second, ask the advisor about their training, years of experience, education, and designations. What is their investment track record and philosophy? Do they share your values and understand you and your goals? Ask for a list of clients you can speak with. And, finally, go with your gut.

CHAPTER 8

Retirement Accounts

The "golden years" is a public relations term for that time in your life when your hair might be white or gray, you do not have to set your alarm clock to get up in the morning, and you get to reinvent yourself and have some fun.

People who have access to some kind of pension plan or retirement fund can enjoy traveling, recreating, spoiling family, or even taking on a new enterprise. Some who might have done a little saving for retirement and reach the age of 65, or 67 if you were born after 1960, can consider their Social Security income as extra money not essential for daily living expenses. The group no one wants to be in is the one that has little or nothing set aside for retirement because the monthly payment from Social Security, between $1,000 and $2,500, almost certainly is not going to be enough to live on.

Such scenarios have implications for your estate plan. Most retirement planning sets a target for how much money you think you will need when you retire so you can finally stop working. However, that plan is an estimate, and things can happen that mean you have more or less money than you need.

As the Great Recession taught us, income does not necessarily commensurate with the cost of living, and investments can be unstable. Even if your basic planning escaped the economic havoc, you might have still found yourself at age 70 guardian of your grandchildren. Or your trip to Mongolia was an absolute blast, but it ended when you fell off a camel and broke a leg. Now, you have physical therapy bills piling up. Planning requires imagining contingencies.

Your Nest Egg

Depending on the kinds of investment strategies you follow, the money you set aside for retirement is yours to keep or lose. Looking at the retirement savings plans you have is part of the estate inventory you will find in *Chapter 10*. But some basic knowledge about what retirement resources people often have is a good place to begin. You might decide you need to make some changes or want to add a new method of saving.

You probably already know the basic parameters of your retirement plan if it is provided through your employment. The human resources department at your company might have mandated a meeting every time a policy change was implemented, and plan descriptions and reports are periodically distributed. However, what this information means within the context of estate planning is different than simply deciding how much money to take out of your paycheck every week.

Different companies offer different types of retirement plan options, and these have changed dramatically over time. Besides changing tax laws, many companies have scaled back their participation in retirement plans or even stopped offering the benefit. Once a virtually guaranteed benefit, pension plans and employer contributions to employee retirement accounts are no longer certain.

Knowing the kind of retirement program in which you participate and the obligations, if any, of the entity offering that plan is important. Professional associations and various government agencies also have retirement plans available, but their plans tend to be different than private employers' plans. Once you know which type of plan you have, you can determine how it fits into your estate plan. It is one of the assets your advisor will need to consider.

Employer pension plans

This list of pension plans is not exhaustive. Chat with your estate-planning people after getting an overview from this section.

Pension and 401(k) plans are the most common ways employers provide a retirement benefit for their employees.

A pension plan is a program set up by an employer, including a government agency, to provide money to pay employee benefits upon retirement. Each employee has an individual account or vested interest, and the employer makes a contribution to each employee's account based on the terms of the plan.

There are two common types of pension plans. One is a defined benefit plan from which the employee will receive a specified amount of money upon retirement. The amount of the disbursement made is based on the number of years of employment. The second is a defined contribution plan, which sets a specific percentage of income, the employee will put into the plan and makes payments only in the amount of money an employee has contributed to the plan. Some of these plans include an employer match.

A qualified pension plan means the amount of money that the employer puts into an employee's account is not taxed as income during the fiscal year the contribution is made. The income is tax-deferred. The employee pays taxes on that money when he or she receives it in the form of a monthly pension payment. Employee contributions to these accounts are made on a pretax basis.

The following conditions might exist:

- **Cost-of-living adjustment:** Some plans will have a variable that will allow for annual increases in the payments made to the employee to help cover the cost of rising prices. Not all plans have this feature.

- **Joint-with-survivor pension:** When an employee dies, her benefits will be paid to her spouse for the remainder of his life. If the spouse waives that right, the employee's pension payments will be larger because there is no requirement to set aside extra money for future payments to a spouse and the pension payments end when the employee dies.

- **Survivor benefit:** A portion of the deceased employee's pension is paid to the surviving spouse. The terms of the pension plan rules set the amount, which is frequently a percentage.

- **Waiver:** A written statement signed by a spouse declining the right to receive benefits. This waiver must be signed to legally sever the right to claim any benefits. An alternative agreement, such as a prenuptial agreement, will not be enough.

- **Limits:** There can be some maximum annual payouts on some pension plans.

Distributing profits or shares of the company's stock is a way for a company to avoid putting cash into a retirement fund. With a profit-sharing plan, employees receive a portion of the profits the company earned. The plan determines the amount that will be contributed to each employee's account. The funds can also be used to invest in programs for components such as a disability or medical plan.

An employer establishes stock bonus plans to give shares of a company's stock to employees. When the employee receives the shares, he must pay taxes based on the value of the stock. An ESOP is a kind of stock bonus plan. The employer contributes shares of its stock to a qualified trust, and the employees only pays taxes based on distributions they receive.

Before employees can receive any distributions or take full ownership of a pension plan, employees have to be vested. They must meet the predetermined requirements for the number of years they have worked for the employer.

Many employers set up a scale of ownership based on the number of years served. For example, if you only work for the company for two years, you are not vested, but when you reach three years, you become 15 percent vested. You can take ownership of 15 percent of the company's contribution to your pension plan plus whatever funds you have contributed. Over time, the percentage of your ownership increases, and at any percent vested above zero, you will be able to take your contributions and the vested percentage you have achieved.

More common today is the 401(k) plan. The equivalent of this plan for nonprofit entities is the 403(b) plan. Named after the IRS code number defining this kind of plan, the 401(k) allows your employer to automatically make contributions through deductions from your paycheck. The advantage is the money is taken out before taxes, so the amount you pay in taxes is reduced. You will still have to pay taxes on that money and the interest it earns until you withdraw money from the account. The employer can make a matching tax-deferred contribution to your account. You can take the plan with you when you leave an employer, but the funds must be invested into another approved retirement plan within 60 days or you will pay taxes. Also, the percentage of the employer contribution you can take with you will likely depend on the vesting schedule for that plan.

Before talking about how you get all this retirement money, look at a few other retirement options.

IRAs and Then Some

Individuals can use a retirement plan option that some companies use. An annuity is an investment that you create by contributing a specific amount of money over a predetermined period of time with a fixed rate of return for a number of years. The money you put into an annuity is not tax-deductible or taken pretax from your paycheck if it is an employer-sponsored plan. A distribution made to the annuity beneficiary will be for a fixed term, or a specific number of years. The distributions will begin at a predetermined date, typically the year you retire, so you will be in a lower income tax bracket and the distributions will be subject to income tax. The interest on the annuity is accumulated tax-free but will be taxed upon distribution. Here is an example:

In 2008, Rob purchases an annuity from an insurance company for $60,000. The terms of the agreement stipulate Rob will fund the annuity with 10 annual payments of $6,000. For 10 years, starting in 2018, Rob will receive $9,000 a year from the annuity. In 2018, Rob will retire, and his tax bracket will be lower than when he was working full-time. Now he will pay lower taxes on that money.

Those annual payments Rob will receive beginning in 2018 will include the income he earned from the annual premiums he paid, which accumulated tax-free while the annuity was being funded. The only taxable portion of each $9,000 annuity payment Rob gets will be $3,000 because $6,000 of that came from the premium payments he made to fund the annuity. For a $60,000 investment, the final value of the annuity will be $90,000.

The return on this investment is low, so it appeals to people who do not feel comfortable with an investment strategy with a higher risk. A variable annuity is based on the same concept, but the funds are invested in the stock market, so the return depends on how well or poorly the economy does.

If you are self-employed, there is a retirement savings plan for you as well. The Keogh plan, pronounced "key-oh," is a qualified retirement plan for sole proprietors and partners, but your employees can also use it. The restrictions, distributions, and other details are similar to a defined-contribution plan or defined-benefit plan.

An individual retirement arrangement (IRA) is just what it sounds like: a retirement account you set up for yourself. There is a limit to the contributions you can make annually. There is a tax deduction for making these contributions every year, so they technically are tax-free contributions. The taxes come after you withdraw the money. You are probably earning less at this time, so the amount you pay will be lower, which is one of the main selling points for this kind of retirement investment. You can hold onto these funds until 70 and a half, but after that, the payments will begin.

The next generation of the IRA is called the Roth IRA. Named after its primary legislative sponsor, Senator William Roth from Delaware, this IRA's contributions are also tax-deductible in the year they are made, and taxes are paid when the money is withdrawn. The difference here is the interest earned while the money is invested will be tax-free if you own the Roth IRA for at least five years. There are limitations on how you can invest the money in your Roth account, and there are big penalties if you take the money out before five and a half years have elapsed, but you can begin distributions that early if you meet the conditions. This IRA also has a distribution requirement that kicks in at age 70 and a half.

Your Government Nest Egg

Social Security, Medicare, Medicaid: Most people have heard the terms and been told this is a safety net for those who have absolutely no other resources on which to rely when they are no longer able to work or are legally entitled to receive government benefits. That regular Federal Insurance Contributions Act (FICA) deduction, painfully visible on every pay stub you have ever received, makes up these government benefits.

The Social Security Administration now sends out annual reports that break down your contributions and estimate the payment that you are likely to receive. If you are not getting one, you can go to **www.ssa.gov** and find out why. Even if you have not yet seen one of those statements, it is safe to assume it will not be enough to pay all your bills when you retire. It is still important to understand how much of your money the government will give back to you and how it will affect your taxes and the taxes your beneficiaries will pay. Social Security benefits are taxable income.

Social Security retirement benefits

The retirement income Social Security provides depends on how many years you worked full time and paid into the system. If you meet the minimums of 10 years of employment or 40 quarter-years, you are considered to be fully insured. Those who have less than the minimum time, such as younger people or those who have worked on and off over a long period of time, are called currently insured and are entitled to disability benefits only.

You can begin receiving these payments at 65 or 67 if you were born after 1960. If you decide to work while receiving benefits, the amount you receive can be reduced. There is an earnings limit for various age ranges. However, if you defer receiving your benefit until later in your life, for example at 69 or 70, your payments will increase.

Your Social Security payments do not have to be paid directly to you. You can designate a beneficiary for the full benefit or split it between you and another person. One-half of your payment can go to your current spouse, or you can designate an ex-spouse to whom you were married for at least 10 years who has not remarried. Children can also receive half the payment while you are alive or 75 percent of the payment after you die; adopted children qualify, and under some circumstances, a stepchild might also qualify. Grandchildren and widows or widowers can also receive benefits as long as they meet specific criteria.

Part of this benefit is a lump sum to the surviving spouse or child of the deceased to help with funeral expenses.

Social Security disability benefit

If you are unable to work and you qualify as disabled, you can receive Social Security disability payments until you reach 65. There is a list of disabilities that according to the government definition of the word qualifies or disqualifies you. At 65, you begin to receive the Social Security retirement benefit at the same rate. The amount of money you receive depends on your work history. You can find more information at **www.ssa. gov/disability**.

Social Security Supplemental Security Income (SSI)

This benefit is for people who have little property or are blind or disabled in some other way. This is an absolute last resort. It is there if you need it, but doing everything possible to avoid that need is an excellent idea.

Medicare and Medicaid

These terms are not interchangeable even though they both are a medical benefit. Medicare is a medical insurance program the federal government offers to people who are 65 or older, certain disabled people under the age of 65, and anyone with permanent kidney failure. This last criterion was added in 1972 out of a concern that people needing life-sustaining dialysis might not be able to afford it. Part A of this coverage is hospital insurance, and Part B is medical insurance. Part B now comes with a monthly premium.

Medicaid, or Medi-Cal in California, is state run but supported by federal funding and provides minimal medical benefits for the financially needy. To qualify for this plan, you can only possess property worth a set dollar amount, commonly $2,000. This is the limit in California for an unmarried resident, but different states set different caps for single and married people. There are also categories for the disabled, the elderly, pregnant women, and those living in poverty. Because medical bills can be costly, it is possible a serious illness could devastate your savings and make it necessary to take advantage of this program, so it is important to be aware that it is available if needed.

Protecting Your Eggs

Estate planning is about protecting your property, and that includes the nest eggs and the baskets that hold them. In addition to estimating what money you will be spending from your retirement accounts, you need to consider what might or might not be left in those accounts after you die. You need to do some additional research with your experts' assistance to make sure what you expect will be there.

Is your pension plan insured?

The Pension Benefit Guarantee Corporation (PBGC) is a federal agency that can insure and therefore protect some or all of your pension if your plan qualifies for the coverage and your company purchases the insurance. Not all pensions are insured and, if they are, it might only be for a percentage of each account. You should contact your employer's human resources office to find out more information on whether your pension is insured and, if so, at which level.

Lump sum payments

Be wary of any retirement investment that offers a lump sum instead of annual distributions. This kind of plan assumes the company will be in business and have the necessary funds when you retire. However, the way formerly indestructible investment institutions and financial companies have failed has proved there is no guarantee. But lump sum distribution might be worth considering if the future stability of the plan is in question for any reason. You might be able to roll it over into a personal account or a trust.

Company stock contributions

If your company matches your retirement investments with their own stock, it is a good idea to diversify your holdings as much as possible. If selling your company stock is an option, most likely after you are fully vested, consider doing that. Company loyalty is important, but risking your financial security on one company is a dangerous investment strategy. Think of WorldCom, Enron, and Bear Stearns. It is not about your commitment to your employer but your responsibility for your own future. When selling your own company's stock, however, be careful about insider trading rules. Get expert legal advice before committing to these transactions.

Medicare supplemental insurance

Medicare is a wonderful benefit, but it is not perfect. There could be times when Medicare will not pay for some treatments, medications, or doctors you need. If you have health issues, it might be a good idea to investigate and invest in Medigap insurance — an insurance plan specifically designed to pay for Medicare exclusions.

Beneficiaries and their taxes

Always name beneficiaries for any retirement resources you have. If you do not name a beneficiary and a substitute, the money in those accounts will be added to your probate estate and be subject to creditors' claims and state and federal government taxation. Also, make sure your beneficiaries know they have been named and are informed of what the tax implications might be if they receive those funds. You might decide to make sure your estate provides them with enough money to cover the taxes. *This was discussed further in Chapter 4.*

Retirement and Estate-Planning Strategy

Now you have an idea of the breadth and scope of retirement savings plans and the resources available to you through the U.S. government, you need to decide how you want to use or save that retirement money.

You can decide to spend it all. You might have saved those retirement funds with the intention of completely exhausting them. That way, you do not have to worry about paying the bills when you want to stick your toes in the sand. Your remaining property is your backup plan. Whatever is left when you die is what you leave to others.

The frugal approach is to choose to link your retirement needs and spending with your estate planning so you estimate what you will need until you die, and then add a cushion to preserve the bulk of your estate for your spouse, children, grandchildren, and others.

By using this last approach, you take into account tax payments and future security for the people and organizations that mean the most to you. This is much more work and adds other considerations, such as inflation and changing tax laws. But it is your money, and this is the best way to have a say in what happens to it when you no longer have a voice.

CASE STUDY: RETIREMENT ACCOUNTS AND ESTATE PLANNING

Howard McEwen, CFA
Makris Financial Group, Inc.

How much of an impact does a retirement account have on an overall estate plan?

A will does not dictate the beneficiary of retirement plans such as 401(k) and IRAs.

The owner of each of those types of plans is allowed to designate a beneficiary. The 401(k) or IRA's custodial agreement lays out how the beneficiaries are treated. This custodial agreement overrides anything a will has to say.

Owners should do and look for the following:

- Make sure they designate a primary beneficiary who gets the money when you die.
- Make sure they designate a contingent beneficiary who gets the money if you die and your primary beneficiary is also dead.
- Make sure the custodial agreement allows a per stirpes designation. Per stirpes means if one beneficiary dies, that beneficiary's heirs will be entitled to those assets.

- If needed, make sure beneficiary restrictions can be put in place. If someone is young or has special needs, getting a large chunk of money at your death might not be the best thing for them.

- Regularly review beneficiaries and make sure you have records of who they are. Let your heirs know where they can find those records.

Any negative impact on estate planning is not tremendous if the retirement accounts are managed properly. The primary thing is to keep beneficiary designations updated.

For example, my client Johnny Jones, who came to my office several years ago, is a widower in his late 70s. He had a daughter and two sons. His daughter, Irene, was married with two children. His eldest son, Max, was married with three children. Bob, the baby of the family, never married and had no children. Bob also had some brushes with the law and is still wrestling with addiction problems.

Johnny retired from a large Fortune 500 company after more than 30 years of work. His main asset was his 401(k) plan that he rolled over into an IRA when he retired. Johnny did not give much consideration to designating a beneficiary. In fact, he did not remember discussing it with his advisor.

After growing dissatisfied with his old advisor, Johnny came to my firm. His eldest son Max had died in an industrial accident three years previously. I noticed on his current statements Max was still listed as a beneficiary.

"Yeah, I just hadn't gotten to that yet," said Johnny.

After looking over the custodial agreement, I explained what would happen to Johnny's money if he happened to die without updating it.

"The custodial agreement doesn't provide a per stirpes provision," I told him. "What this means is that if you die right now, only Irene and Bob will get any money. Max's children will be totally disinherited."

"You mean, even though he's still on there, his share won't pass on to his kids?"

"Right," I said. I explained the court might award inheritance to Max's children if Irene and Bob decided to disclaim, or turn down, a portion, but there was no guarantee Irene and Bob or the courts would carry out his wishes in this case.

"Also, how will inheriting a large sum of money affect Bob? He's already dealing with addiction issues. Could getting this inheritance actually kill him?"

These are blunt questions with a simple answer: Keep an updated beneficiary designation form, designate those beneficiaries per stirpes, and restrict the kind of money Bob would inherit.

Is there anything a person can do to maximize their retirement plans?

I consider two ways to maximize a client's retirement plan. First is before death by properly allocating a client's account according to their risk-reward profile. The second is after death.

Here is how: In the custodial agreement of the IRA or 401(k), they should verify their beneficiaries can perform a stretch IRA.

For the majority of Americans, an IRA or 401(k) is their largest asset. By stretching that IRA across multiple generations, an IRA owner can create tremendous wealth for future generations of his family.

How do you stretch an IRA? By simply withdrawing the absolute minimum necessary to meet IRS regulations. The funds that remain in the IRA are allowed to compound tax-deferred over a number of years.

Here is a simple example:

David Johansen is married to Patty. They have one son, Sami. Sami has a daughter, Chrissie, age 1, who is the apple of her grandparents' eyes.

Sami is financially self-sufficient, so David designates Chrissie as the sole primary beneficiary on one of his IRAs that Patty will not need if he should die.

In the year David turns 70 and a half, the IRS mandates he withdraw a percentage of his IRA. This is so they can take it. In that first year, the withdrawal is 3.65 percent.

David takes this withdrawal and then dies.

Chrissie becomes the owner of that IRA now worth $100,000. Because it was her grandfather's IRA, she is still required to make withdrawals, but those withdrawals are based on her age, not her grandfather's.

That first year, 1-year-old Chrissie would have to withdraw $1,225. The IRS tables provide a life expectancy of 81.6 years for Chrissie, so $100,000 / 81.6 years = $1,225. If the IRA earns an average of 8 percent over Chrissie's life expectancy, her grandfather's IRA would have paid her $8,167,629.

State Capitol building in Sacramento, California, USA

CHAPTER 9
Setting Priorities

Estate planning is more than just deciding what to do with your stuff after your death. Some thought needs to go into what you want to do and how you want to try to prepare for the things you can and cannot predict. You might wish for a crystal ball for looking into the future, but an even better resource is close at hand — the past. By making time to review the decisions and choices you have already made in your life, you will be able to see what has been important to you.

When you had an opportunity to invest in your 401(k) at work, did you put in the maximum amount allowable, contribute a modest percentage of your income, or defer investing until later? Are you glad you made the choice you did, or would you do things differently based on what you know now?

The answers you come up with are an example of how to begin making some decisions. By comparing against your present situation what you thought about financial matters, the people who were in your life, and the organizations you supported, you will be able to see patterns or inconsistencies that are important in setting priorities for your estate.

This review also needs to include your current financial situation. Your view on credit card use influences the credit card debt you have or lack. If you do not have any credit cards, that says something about what you think about the use of plastic for making purchases and whether paying interest on a purchase is acceptable. Maybe you have a small balance because in the same month you replaced the tires on your car or the bottom of the water heater decided to drop out and you simply did not have the cash to pay for a new one. Whether you paid off that balance right away or let it ride for a bit until you got back from your following business trip also says something.

It can be fun to reminisce about the unexpected adventure to South America with a college course you only took because of someone you thought you wanted to date. It can also be difficult, even painful, to remember a family beach vacation that ended with Grandpa in the hospital and dying three months later. But if you make the effort, you might be able to recall how much fun he had preparing for and involving you and the other children in the crab boil at sunset, and that will inspire a desire to share that experience with your grandchildren.

The essential part of this process is being attentive to the insignificant, the significant, and everything in between. All these details can serve as helpful pointers now and potential visions for the future.

Your Own Who's Who

Even though every person in your life might not end up in your will, considering the people who are important to you and those who are not is one way to identify what matters most to you. Because you are considering your priorities for yourself in addition to your family, friends, and maybe even professional associates, a review of people connected to those priorities makes sense.

The most obvious important people are your family and closest friends. Most people can rattle off the names of people they are related to by birth, marriage, or mutual agreement for friends who became chosen family. A bit more thought might be needed when considering extended family or distant relatives.

Family might be so important to you that everyone living in your house sits down to eat at least one meal, often dinner, together every day. Children home from college or grandparents visiting from out of state for a week all know this is expected. Your children might also know there are some family members they never see but for whom everyone signs the family holiday card each year. If those same people send a note with a small gift for a birthday or graduation, your family would send a thank-you note because those distant relatives are equally important. These relatives are always invited to parties even though they never come.

Priorities revealed:

- Time with family is more than important; it is essential.

- Every celebration that calls for a party begins with a call to family members to find out which dates work for them.

- Even though some relatives live far away or might even be reclusive, you make sure your children keep in touch; you want them to have a strong sense of family regardless of proximity.

Implications for estate planning:

- Immediate family is so important you want to make sure they have what they need.

- You desire to leave something to every family member whether cash or a memento.

- Is everyone clear about how important your family is to you? Just because family time and ties are important to you does not mean your siblings, children, or anyone else will be aware of this. Clearly communicating this priority to your family is a good idea. When the will is read and the distant relatives are included, your wishes are carried out, and the immediate family does not contest your bequests.

People come and go from our lives at various times for different reasons. The people with whom you surround yourself now are probably a different mix than the people from your past. Even though life circumstances play a part in the coming and going of people, the effort you make to include or exclude people from your life places a value on that relationship. Going out of your way to call someone or delete a message from the answering machine with no intention of calling the person back says something about how you feel about that individual.

Looking at the changes in your personal circle is one way to approach this review of people. For example, after being widowed, you might have lost touch with your in-laws; this does not bother you because they never liked you or the fact that you married their son or daughter. The children are old enough to go visit their grandparents when they want to.

You remarried and have become close to the extended family of your current husband or wife. This new, blended family includes an alcoholic uncle you simply cannot stand to be around even though everyone thinks he is the life of every party. Similarly, when your children get married, they do not want to have to juggle multiple Thanksgiving dinners because they embrace the blended family as positive and open. They propose a huge family gathering of all sides that results in meeting new family members with whom you begin to enjoy weekend camping trips and a weekly bowling league.

Priorities revealed:

- You want to have people in your life with whom you can have a friendly, healthy relationship.

- You are willing to meet familial obligations, such as making an effort with your in-laws when your wife was alive, but once an obligation is fulfilled, you are all right with letting it go.

- Distancing yourself from people who can be harmful to you or your family is also all right, but you try to do it in a manner that does not upset others.

- Family is important but not exclusive; Events for biological family only rarely happen because they feel exclusionary.

Implications for estate planning:

- Including people who are not related by blood in your will must be handled legally and carefully to avoid any contest after you are gone. State laws governing family inheritance are clear; the same cannot be said for nonrelatives.

- Leaving money to a family member with an addiction or some other life problem, such as an abusive spouse or unscrupulous children, might require the use of a trust and a trustee to avoid the potential disasters that can result.

- Give some consideration to not including someone in your will. Giving a significant bequest to a specific person might not sit well with you, but consider a small gift to avoid a contest due to complete exclusion.

The faces of people you call friends can also change over time. For example, Debbie, a friend from elementary school with whom you kept in touch through letters when you lived in different states, is now a neighbor thanks to her job transfer. The college roommate with whom you shared many late-night study sessions and burnt microwave popcorn went from experimenting with drugs to hardcore use. The last time he called you to bail him out of jail, you told him it was the last time, and you have not heard from him since.

There are also the people we encounter just doing our everyday business. We can easily take them for granted and not realize their importance until something happens. For example, there is Betty, the elderly woman who lives down the street and has no family. She ends up in a nursing home after breaking her hip, which ends your Friday morning visits for tea and cookies. There is the librarian who knows you by name and suggests books you might like. And there is the mechanic who normally changes the oil in your car but is not there one day when you stop in. His son is at the register and explains he was feeling tired and needed a few days off.

Priorities revealed:

- Your awareness of and concern for others extends beyond your immediate circle to acquaintances.

- Frequenting local shops and businesses is important to you; you go out of your way to avoid large impersonal stores.

- You prefer to be a part of the community in which you live.

- Neighbors matter.

Implications for estate planning:

- Add to your list of bequests the organizations and institutions you appreciate and that have been a source of friendships for you, such as your local library. Support them when you are no longer around to cast your vote for a levy or make a donation.

- The support you give to a family owned business might not be significant, but something in your estate might help them. Your mechanic might appreciate the tools you use for fixing your car.

- Donating your book collection to the local library would make your family happy; they are not big readers, and it would be one less thing to handle when it comes time to sell the house.

By taking time to consider people, you will naturally think of memories and specific milestones in life that are related. The things you experience directly or simply witness also provide an opportunity to review your priorities.

Memory Lane

Looking back to the mundane as well as the amazing through the filter of estate planning makes it possible to see how the past can inform and even direct the future. If you see accumulated knowledge and financial resources as the means to adding some adventure and comfort to the later years in your life, not just as gifts for others, you can live unfulfilled dreams or expand on some wonderful experiences.

Consider that trip to South America. Would you have begged, borrowed, or gone into debt to have the extra month in the rainforest if you knew you might never have the chance to go back? Look at this year's vacation plan. Are you going anywhere near a rainforest? Would you consider changing your plans to return to that place south of the border? Are you disappointed that you cannot change your plans? Would you like to go again if you could come up with the money for the trip? Or has the idea of some tropical disease soured you on that kind of adventure? Does a cruise ship that anchors off the coast and includes a one-day trip to the edges of the greenery sound more like your idea of fun?

There are any number of events from the past that underscore the priorities you had at that time and how far you have drifted into another view of what is important. Here are a few memory joggers to get you thinking:

Family time:

- Were vacations with immediate family only or large, extended gatherings?

- Was the annual visit from the cousins fun or torture?

- Did having a sleepover at a friend's house made you want to stay there or go home?

- Did Thanksgiving dinner include a children's table?

- How many parties were held at your house, and which ones did you enjoy or loathe?

School:

- Which was your favorite subject or class?

- How did a memorable teacher get you excited about learning?

- How did you handle the class bully when it was your turn to be picked on?

- Were you public or private? Liked or disliked? Why?

- Did you participate in science fairs by choice or force? What was your level of desire to hide under your display table during judging?

- Were you in a fraternity or sorority, or were you an independent thinker?

- Did you hold class office positions, either by election or appointment?

Extracurricular:

- Did you participate in scouting or make fun of Scouts?

- Were you a reporter for the school paper?

- Did you play in the band?

- Did you help teachers clean after school?

- Were you a member of any clubs?

- Did you play sports?

Things you would do over:

- Marrying your first, second, or third spouse

- Rehabbing the cute bungalow that ended up selling for less than you paid

- Studying economics and only taking one art class in college

- Giving up your film cameras for digital

- Donating your turntable and all your jazz records

- Not touring Europe before having children

These life experiences are more than just a reflection of how you used to feel or what your parents forced you into doing. Your recollections and the way you respond to them now are a measure of what matters to you now.

Maybe that beach house you rented in 1998 is exactly the kind of home you wanted to have when you dreamed of living in a beach house. Perhaps that dream is never going to come true because of the circumstances of your life, but there is still time to make changes right now. For example, you have eight more years until you are fully vested in your pension fund, so you have eight years to plan. Prepare to sell your existing home in the suburbs; help your children deal with the shock of your move to Nags Head, North Carolina; and get your finances in order. Your accountant and lawyer can get to work on the papers for the living trust you need to make sure your retirement years will be nonstop beach time.

If having fun in your life was something you passed up to fulfill obligations or deferred to achieve other goals, you might decide recreation is so critical you want to share that lesson with your grandchildren. One way to do that is to make sure they have the money necessary to fund the fun, Set up a mad money trust for each grandchild to do whatever they want in the summer between high school and college. Once you make that a priority because their parents have already funded their tuition and other fees, you can figure out how much you need to save or how much you need to avoid spending from your retirement account to fund those trusts.

Reminiscing often includes groups of people with similar views and dreams. Those groups also matter when it comes to estate planning.

Your "People"

Not everyone has an entourage of groupies, support staff, and employees to do their bidding. More often, you are the one doing the work, and frequently it is for a nonprofit organization. Your priorities about which causes or institutions to support have most likely changed over the years. The arts, once a luxury on a limited budget, are now at the top of your annual giving list, but the peace center that was struggling to survive in the basement of the dilapidated building next to your first apartment has moved to the storefront and still gets 20 hours of your time every month.

The institutions that rely on your time, money, or donations of office supplies have captured your imagination or hopes or maybe just inspired you with their underdog determination. Whatever the reason, they are important to you. Although they consider you among their supporters, or as on of their people, the fact is your desire to see them succeed makes them your people.

Considering the nonprofits you have supported at different times in your life might spark an interest to get involved or lend support again. Life changes; a parent dying of cancer might inspire you to add the American Cancer Society or a hospice to the list of charities you wish to support.

Because estate planning is more than distributing belongings after you die, factor the importance you place on these groups into your priorities. The peace center maybe is on the verge of needing to move because they are growing so rapidly. Or that old bakery building you bought a few years ago has perhaps not turned out to be the successful investment property your real estate agent swore it would be. Putting it into a charitable trust or making an outright donation of it to the peace center might be the best way to help them and reduce the amount of real property in your estate.

If you do move to that beach house in Nags Head, the time you spend at the cat rescue shelter is no longer going to be an option. You know they desperately need volunteers, but even more desperate is a need for cat food. A donation of cash for the purchase of food is only going to be possible if you set up a way to make it happen.

After you fund the mad money trusts, make sure you have enough to live on during retirement and cover the cost of your disability insurance as the safety net. After that, it might be that you only have enough in your estate to support two charities. Will you choose the arts organizations, the peace center, or the cat shelter? Do you want to set aside a little extra in case you find some institution in Nags Head that you want to support later?

These are the difficult decisions that must be made if you prefer not to work extra hours or cut into your current spending to allow for future expenditures.

Must-Do

Some people are inspired to create a must-do list after considering the things they never thought they would get to do in this lifetime or the envious moments they spent listening to others describe what you they always dreamed about doing. Be it mountain climbing, scuba diving, going out to dinner at a five-star restaurant, or taking two weeks off work to just stay at home and relax, the things you feel are important enough to put on a list are important enough to make happen.

Setting priorities for your estate planning is a means to that must-do end. Identifying what matters most right now and what you thought was important but now realize is no big thing makes it possible to consider financial decisions that will have an impact now and later.

CASE STUDY: A FINANCE COACH FOR ESTATE PLANNING

Sue Holm, Founder
Make Peace with Money
sue@makepeacewithmoney.com

How should a person make decisions about their priorities?

Make all major decisions about financial priorities with a trusted advisor or counselor. For some folks, that can be family or friends. For some, that is a financial planner or advisor. If someone has emotional issues about money, he or she should consult a financial counselor, coach, or therapist who is comfortable with money issues.

An element of spirituality also touches these decisions during life and when contemplating death. How much to give away? To whom? Why? When? Charitable giving; tithing, or donating a fixed percentage of income to a religious institution; and giving back are all rich issues for discussion among families, faith communities, and in our world. Does charity begin at home? What does that mean? What does that look like? Is money good, bad, or neutral? Are money and spirituality linked or not?

How do people apply those priorities to their decisions about disbursing their money and property after their death?

By not planning, people allow the state to dictate the distribution of their money and property. For those who have priorities, familial or spiritual, those priorities will drive the nature of the disbursal.

Why do people fight over things such as a toaster or a chair after someone has died?

Because they have unresolved emotional issues either about themselves and their self-worth or their relationship with the deceased.

How can the person who owns the toaster or chair prepare his family for that situation?

If people are clear about their intentions in creating estate plans and have the occasion to discuss their intent with their family, it can defuse some of the tension. The person who owns things can create an atmosphere in which it is all right to ask for what you want while they are still alive. They can ask their loved ones what they need or want as a remembrance. They can create a system to disbursing things not otherwise specified in the will.

How often should those priorities be revisited?

Financial priorities should be revisited at all major life milestones: marriage, divorce, birth of children, children turning 18, and birth of grandchildren.

What are the benefits of working with a financial counselor or coach?

The benefits include financial clarity, mastery, and ultimately peace with money. This manifests in decreasing debt, increasing saving, and earning what you are worth.

Many people do not know financial counseling or coaching is available. Many people with financial issues know they need help but do not know how to find it. A lot of people think because they are smart and successful in most areas of their life, they should already know what to do with money or will be able to figure it out themselves. This can be increasingly frightening and frustrating as they try and fail on their own.

Among the most productive discussions between a financial counselor and client are those that involve the differentiation between needs and wants and how to prioritize them.

How should a financial professional collaborate with other people in an estate-planning team?

During the financial counseling process, the counselor will refer the client to an estate-planning professional if the client does not yet have an estate plan.

Financial counselors can be an excellent resource for estate-planning professionals working with surviving spouses or partners who need or want some structure and support while they assume financial responsibility for themselves or for the estate.

Additionally, estate-planning professionals should consider referring clients who inherit sums of money or assets they are inexperienced in managing to a financial counselor.

How does a person choose a financial professional? Which characteristics and experience should a client look for?

As this is not a licensed or regulated field, it is important clients examine the credentials of anyone they are considering as a financial counselor or coach. Training agencies, such as the Financial Recovery Institute (**www.financialrecovery.com**), frequently list those counselors or coaches who have been trained and certified.

Many clients seeking financial counseling have not talked about their money issues with anyone. They frequently have conscious and subconscious money secrets. It is imperative clients trust their financial counselor, and a financial counselor or coach should be able to deal with the client's emotional issues that underlie the money issues.

CHAPTER 10

Choosing Who, What, How, When, and Why

Now that you know what you own or need to save and have an idea of what you will need to keep for yourself as you go forward and a sense of the people and organizations you would like to support with your hard-earned assets, it is time to put all that information together into a comprehensive estate plan. The detailed overview of the choices you have for delivering assets provided in *Chapters 5-8* is just that — an overview. The legal restrictions and limitations of different kinds of trusts, annuities, insurance policies, and other financial vehicles will help you identify potential resources that will meet your goals. Only professionals in estate planning are going to be able to make your estate plan meet your goals and be legally binding.

Beyond the difficult choices of who gets what, you also need to choose the CPAs, lawyers, financial advisors, insurance agents, and others who will be a part of your estate-planning and management team. Many of these people receive commissions for the sale of different kinds of products. The trust that might be best for you could have a smaller commission than the trust with plenty of extras, but a planner who is doing his or her job will suggest what is best for your needs, not his or her checking account. Even though a less expensive firm might be attractive while you are still building up your estate, consider the longevity of the firm. There is the distinct possibility that later you will have a larger estate if you get proper guidance.

Something with such a long-term impact as your estate planning deserves a high level of care, thought, and attention.

Who and When: The Matching Game

The card game Memory, or Concentration, involves placing all the cards in a deck upside down on a table in a grid. Each player turns over two cards. If they do not match, the player flips them back over, and the next player takes a turn. The goal is to keep flipping over cards and remembering where each one is so you can make matches. When all the matches are found, the player with the most sets of matches wins. It is a good way to teach children how to increase their concentration skills, but the premise of the game is also a good method for distributing your estate. The key difference is that you decide what makes a match.

If you are unsure of how to begin, consider the sticky note method. Put the name of each person and institution you wish to support with your estate on a note. Include yourself in that list if you plan on creating a living trust or dedicating other resources to your retirement that will be a part of your estate plan. In the case of multiple beneficiaries, for example when you benefit from a living trust during your life and have a beneficiary for that trust after your death, be sure to note both people.

Make a sticky note for each asset that you listed on your estate planning worksheet in Appendix A of this book. Prioritize them by laying them side-by-side to give yourself a better visual of your planning.

Next, get the priorities worksheet found in Appendix A of this book so you can compare what you think you want against the practical structure of the estate you are crafting. Then, lay them all out by matching them up, and see whether the matches are what you want them to be.

Jeanine	Carol	Mary Lynn	Me
Education trust $50,000+ book collection (value =$10k)	Luna Pier Road property $125,000	Trust for travel money $60,000	Trust for retirement funds $900,000
Me now, Danny beneficiary	Grandma Sophie	Peace center	Cat shelter
Living trust for Nags Head beach house $250,000	Trust for assisted-living expenses $500,000	Charitable trust: old bakery on Ludlow Ave. and $10,000	$5,000

This method gives you the chance to see the differences in the amounts, property, and other bequests you make. That side-by-side comparison might also raise questions in your mind about the implications of the distribution.

Carol tends to be a black-and-white kind of person, so she might get upset when she learns the difference in the value of the property she gets and the

Nags Head property going to Danny. The property she gets is worth 50 percent less. The facts that her profession is rehabbing houses and she can invest a small amount to make the property equal, if not higher, in value is something you might want to explain. Or, you might decide to add some cash to her bequest to soften the blow.

You might not feel right about giving Jeanine a $50,000 bequest when Mary Lynn is getting $60,000, even though you know it is what they need. Add a little something to Jeanine's bequest if that makes you feel better.

Or all these differences might not bother you. You know what you are doing and why, and because it is your estate plan, the issue of fairness is a moot point.

Another thing this exercise can do is provide an opportunity to consider bundling or separating items in your estate as part of a bequest. If you are looking only at the dollar value of a gift, packaging together the sentimental items with stocks, bonds, or cash will give you a chance to customize a bequest to the person who receives it.

Mary Lynn is not a reader, so the book collection would not mean as much to her as Jeanine, who is getting her degree in creative writing.

The charitable trust for the peace center that includes the old bakery is an incredibly generous gift — the largest they have ever received. That being said, the actual expense of the upgrades needed to meet building codes will take a big chunk out of their operating budget. The extra $10,000 can be invested until they are ready to do the work, and it is also a way to motivate other donors to kick in some support.

It is not necessary to use sticky notes for this exercise, but it is important to note a light breeze could blow away your efforts. Imagine how an overly enthusiastic pet can scatter pieces of paper that do not stick. A large dry erase board or chalkboard serves the same purpose. Regardless of the method, the ultimate goal is simple: Match up your priorities with the people and gifts you wish to give.

Once you have settled on who is getting what, taking a digital photo of your makeshift plan could help later when you decide you want to make changes. *See Chapter 12 for more information on this.* You will have a record of your notes and can use that to reconstruct and revisit this process, or you maybe will want to show it to a financial advisor. Converting this information to an electronic document is a possibility by using a table in a word processing document or using a spreadsheet program.

An estate plan is something you will need to revisit and change regularly, so consider keeping your notes and other planning documents at least until you are sure you have all the information saved in some other format.

When: Today, Tomorrow, or Later?

An important strategy for estate planning that many do not use is early gifting. The traditional or customary time for distributing an estate is after a person dies, but staying with the traditional can mean a larger estate and more taxes. A gift tax might still apply to the property you hand over early, but given the rate of tax increase, it is possible this could mean a lower tax bill for the beneficiary.

Another thing to consider is when the beneficiary will get the most benefit from the gift you make. Your estate is yours to dispose of how and when you choose; if you want to take advantage of an opportunity to help a relative or charity in need, you can factor that into your estate plan.

Jeanine graduated from high school with an International Baccalaureate (IB) degree through a special education program her high school offered. She has changed her major from creative writing and is now majoring in political science in college. The whole family thinks she is making a bad decision and is too young to understand how she will be limiting her career choices to only politics.

You see the potential Jeanine sees — and more. International corporations, government embassies, and a long list of opportunities await the person who has the background and understanding of multiple cultures and knows how to navigate the intricacies of government policy and social mores.

The cultural club she belongs to is planning a trip to Mongolia, and she desperately wants to go, but her education trust fund will not cover the expenses of the trip. She can legally go on the trip, but she does not have the cash. Because you want to encourage her passion and efforts to get a well-rounded education, not to mention some invaluable experience before graduation, you decide to create an education trust for Jeanine that specifically covers the cost of school-related travel.

Even though Jeanine will not receive any other money from your estate, you can remind yourself that she is getting an immediate benefit that will have long-term implications for her ability to build her own estate. It might be helpful to explain this to her, too.

Choosing to give some gifts early, putting conditions on other gifts, and explaining the logic behind why you are doing these things all need careful consideration. If your family is competitive or has some other characteristics that could inspire resentment or other negative reactions before or after your death you might want to consider sharing your reasoning. This can be done in the form of a letter to each family member that will be opened after your death or at a one-on-one meeting in which you discuss the terms and conditions of your will and estate.

Regardless of how open or confidential you are about your financial matters, remember after you are gone, your ability to explain yourself is limited. When deciding on the timing of your gifts, keep this in mind.

How: The Professionals

There is a host of people from which to choose your estate-planning team. Areas of specialty can get confusing. A CPA can address tax issues, but so can a lawyer who specializes in tax law. Which is better will depend on what your needs are. *Chapter 2 describes the important people making up your estate-planning team.* Please refer to that chapter for a review of the parties.

The best way to determine who can help you with your estate planning is to look at your needs, preferences, and expectations. If the content of this book is the extent of your estate-planning knowledge, you have much to learn before you can adequatley prepare your estate-planning documents. A professional with access to multiple sources of current information written for the consumer and who has the patience to answer questions will be essential for you. Someone who knows what a QTIP is without looking in the glossary might prefer to seek a professional who can provide more detailed information without getting overly technical.

Beyond that, the circumstances of your life and interests are going to impact the time you have to spend, your level of commitment to achieving whatever timetable you set for completion, and the people with whom you work. Traveling across town for meetings might not be possible if you are going to be caring for your 18-month-old twin nieces while your sister goes back to school for a semester.

Some factors to consider before you begin putting together your estate-planning team are:

- **Interest level:** If a root canal without anesthesia sounds more fun than estate planning or if you have a true desire to plan but lack the time to make it happen, you have some sense of how much you want to engage in this process.

  Consider 75 percent of the population does not do comprehensive estate planning before they die, but the U.S. and state governments have enough laws on the books to take control of and benefit from your lifetime of work and savings. Focus on the benefits of this hard work, and consider the good things it can accomplish for you and those who matter most to you.

- **Deadlines:** Which significant milestones are coming up sooner or later?

  If you have a three-month world tour planned for next year, it would be a good idea to get this wrapped up before you leave the country. If you are not going anywhere for the next few years, you can take this at a slower pace.

- **Health issues:** Even if you are healthy right now, your age and family medical history could impact your planning timetable.

  Grandma Nan lived to be 100, but all her sisters died of breast cancer in their 60s, and you are age 24, 48, or 56. Your father-in-law died at 40 of a massive heart attack, and your husband is 48.

- **Family matters:** Collaborative relationships, disagreements, a marriage or birth, long-standing feuds, addiction struggles, help with child care, and everything in between can impact your decision-making and the time you can commit to this process.

The bickering between two siblings might inspire a desire to cut them both out of your will, and a newly married couple means adding one more person — or two, if baby makes three.

- **Charities:** Like families, organizations go through considerable change. Insignificant change, such as changing staff, or significant change, such as building a new facility, could influence your time commitment to estate planning in addition to your giving.

  The Friends Meeting House where you study received the permits and approvals necessary to go forward with the construction of their new building ahead of schedule; instead of breaking ground in five years, they begin in eight months. You might need to revise when they receive the money you have left them.

Once you have made up your mind to follow through with this estate planning you have been avoiding and you know what your schedule looks like, you need to consider the components and status of your belongings. If you are just beginning to build your estate, such a will requires fewer professionals than someone who has 32 years in the workforce and multiple resources to consider. Special circumstances can complicate the process for any estate of any value.

The following offers examples of the many factors that might come into play when developing your estate family.

Family:

Blended

Not legally recognized

Adoption: Domestic or international

Foreign-born spouse

Personal:

Career changes

Multiple relocations: Domestic or overseas

Frequent layoffs

Mental health concerns

Felony arrest(s)

Income:

Structured settlements

Rental property

Inheritance

Royalties

Unemployment

Outgoing:

Child support

Alimony

Elder care for parents

Terminal illness

Consider whether these things affect you or your estate. They might have implications for your budget in addition to being information your estate planner will need to know. The firm you approach might not want to deal with estate issues related to people who are not U.S. citizens.

If you make decisions based exclusively on the fees they charge, you might take a risk with your estate-planning team members. It is possible you will get lucky and stumble across a CPA in the phone book who has your best interest at heart, and even though he has considerable experience, he is willing to charge next to nothing for his expertise because he wants you to keep your money. But the high-priced estate-planning firm, with more credentials than you have ever seen, is not necessarily going to give you the kind of service you need or collaborate with your other estate-planning partners.

The process of selecting the professionals with whom you will work requires some scrutiny of individual professional standards, such as credentials for a CPA, but some general expectations for this group of people can be defined. Consider the following when choosing a professional to help you with your estate plan:

- Do you recognize the name of the school from which he graduated? What does he do to stay current with changes in financial markets?

- How many years of experience does this person have?

- What is the focus or areas of expertise for that experience and the duration in each area?

- Do they have a private practice, group practice, or corporate environment? Find out whether the expertise of others is readily available if a question or problem arises.

- Ask the Better Business Bureau and allied professional associations, such as the American Bar Association (ABA) for lawyers, for complaints, reprimands, or any other questionable business practices.

- Ask about the nature of relationships with the providers of the products the individual or firm offers; ask for a disclosure of commissions and other perks provided to the individual professional or firm.

- Review the website for current clients. Does the list include people with estates similar to yours, or are they wealthy individuals and business owners? A firm that specializes in businesses might do personal estate planning as an aside for those companies, but that is not its area of expertise.

- Talk to previous and current clients or friends and associates who recommend, or are wary of, the person or company.

Once you have a short list of people to interview for your estate-planning team, prepare as much information as possible in advance of your first meeting. This will help you and the professionals you interview quickly determine how they might be able to help you craft your plan.

CASE STUDY: ESTATE-PLANNING CHOICES

Scott J. Malof, CPA/PFS
SS&G Financial Services, Inc.
Certified Public Accountants
and Advisors
www.SSandG.com

What information should a person collect to prepare for this process?

For the estate-planning process, people should begin preparing a snapshot of where they are today. Create a family tree of personal details including ages and health status for immediate family members and those whom you might have to care for, such as an aging parent. Also remember guardian nominations for your minor children, trustee nominations that are part of a will or other estate options, executor nominations to execute your will, separation and divorce agreements, and tax returns for the past couple of years.

This snapshot should include all relevant financial information: listings of assets and liabilities, details of all insurance policies, and current and future income streams. Your financial situation would include a detailed personal balance sheet listing all assets and liabilities, life insurance policy details, other insurance coverage such as disability coverage, and income and expenses now and in the future.

The last piece, and often the most difficult, is your goals and expectations, including legacies.

What are the most overlooked loopholes or opportunities people miss when coordinating the financial aspect of their estate?

Here are a few:

- Not using each spouse's applicable exclusion amount both at the federal and state level. For example, you could leave everything to your spouse.
- Assuming the children can divvy everything up fairly without fighting. This could be a mistake, not an opportunity.
- Not using a gifting plan

How does the power of gifting affect an estate plan?

All individuals can give any other individual up to $12,000 annually without using up their lifetime applicable exclusion amount of $2,000,000. This money is not included in the donor's estate at death.

For example, a couple has two children, two surviving parents, and four grandchildren. This couple could give away $192,000 annually, which is eight people multiplied by $12,000 in gifts multiplied by two donors. If this were done for a period of 20 years, the donors could remove $3.84 million from their estate and exclude the impact of earnings over those years. This could have a taxable federal estate at the highest rate, which is currently 45 percent. This would be a $1,728,000 savings.

The downside to gifting is relinquishing the control over the property. Also, giving large sums of money to minor children does not come without both good and bad ramifications. This is why estate planning can be so hard for so many people. The answers are not always about saving the most money or passing down the most wealth. It truly comes back to meeting a person's wishes.

How do state laws and federal laws affect estate-planning choices?

Federal and state laws have an enormous impact on estate planning. When people are determining where they would like their property to ultimately go, they need to be cognizant of the legal ramifications of their choices. For example, the rules for the transfer of property in a community-property state vary from those in a common-law state. Knowledge of these rules will help people plan accordingly.

Also, much of estate planning includes trying to minimize any transfer taxes that might come due. The amount of potential federal and state estate or gift tax has an enormous impact on the estate plan. For example, a couple with a $10 million estate could easily save over $1 million with some simple estate-planning techniques. If this couple implements a gifting plan over a number of years, the savings possibility goes up substantially. The highest federal estate tax rate is 45 percent. Proper estate management leads to substantial savings.

Confidentiality from the general public and other family members is important to many people. State laws especially govern which information must be made public record through probate or disclosed on a limited basis, such as through trust reporting to beneficiaries. Clients need to determine how much they want the public or their heirs to know about what they have, how they are passing it, and to whom.

CHAPTER 11

*Planning Your Estate: Last Will and Testament
in California*

The laws of each state direct and control specific requirements for drafting valid wills. Although some principles are common, not all states are the same. Obtaining legal counsel to assist you in drafting your last will and testament is always advisable, especially if you have more than one residence in different states or if you draw up your will in a different state than the one in which you live. You sho uld consult an attorney to ensure your will conforms to the proper controlling state law because it will likely differ in various states. Additionally, state laws change from time to time.

It is important to understand California's statutory requirements for valid wills at the time you draft yours. Otherwise, your efforts to bequeath your property could fail. Regardless of what you wrote down as your intent to distribute your property according to "your will," it will be the same as if you wrote nothing. You will have died intestate — without a will. In that event, your property will be distributed according to state law possibly in ways you never imagined and often at greater court costs.

According to current California law, if you are at least 18 and mentally competent to do so, you can make a will in the state of California.

Elements of a Valid California Will

Under California Probate Code (CPC) 6113, the probate courts will recognize a will as validly executed if:

(1) It was executed in California according to California law governing valid wills

(2) It conforms to the Uniform International Wills Act if executed out of the country

(3) It complies with "the law at the time of execution of the place where the will is executed"

(4) "The execution of the will complies with the law of the place where at the time of execution or at the time of death the testator is domiciled, has a place of abode, or is a national"

California law recognizes four types, or forms, of wills: holographic will, fill-in form will, individual typed or printed will, and international will. With the exception of the holographic will, these will types must be witnessed.

What can be devised in a will

CPC 6101 describes the property a testator can devise in his or her will:

(a) "The testator's separate property."

(b) "The one-half of the community property that belongs to the testator under [California law]"

(c) "The one-half of the testator's quasi-community property that belongs to the testator [under California law]"

To whom property can be devised in a will

CPC 6102 provides that a testator "may make a disposition of property to any person, including but not limited to any of the following:"

(a) "An individual"

(b) "A corporation"

(c) "An unincorporated association, society, lodge, or any branch thereof"

(d) "A county, city, city and county, or any municipal corporation"

(e) "Any state, including this state"

(f) "The United States or any instrumentality thereof"

(g) "A foreign country or a governmental entity therein"

Holographic will

A holographic will is a fully handwritten document recognized under CPC 6111. The value of this type of document is that the testator can sit down and write out the entire will without the need for witnesses and notaries. One of the simplest, shortest, and most famous of holographic wills was one that read, "All to wife."

The key to a holographic will is the document must be fully and legibly written out by hand by the person who has died. No part of it can be typed on a computer and printed, typed on a typewriter, spoken on video or audio tape, or physically written by someone else on behalf of the testator. If it is, the will is invalid unless properly signed by the testator and witnessed according to the requirements of other types of valid California wills. The holographic will must be fully written out by hand and signed and dated by the person making the will. Witnesses can still be used and are recommended, but they are not a legal requirement for the holographic will to be valid. Anyone who wants to make a valid will in California can write it out by hand in this way.

The holographic will must still meet the basic requirements of all wills. The person making the will must evidence that he or she is of sound mind, most often by saying so in specific wording, such as, "I am of sound mind and know what I possess and how I want to distribute it upon my death" or, "This is my last will and testament. I am of sound mind, and I freely state how my possessions shall be divided and dispersed upon my death." The point is to make clear you know who you are, what you own, and your own mind as to how you want to dispose of what you own when you die. A will written by someone who is mentally incompetent or under coercion or duress is not valid.

That you want your writing to be considered a will as opposed to a letter, memorandum, journal, reflection, list, or some other nontestamentary document is crucial. If, after your death, someone challenges that your handwritten document is not actually your last will and testament, the court will be obliged to examine it to determine what you intended when you wrote it. Words like, "I declare this document to be my last will and testament," clearly state that you intend the document to be considered your will.

If the first key to a holographic will is intent, the second is that it carries your signature. Along with your handwriting, it is your signature that authenticates the document. It does not have to be at the end of the document although that is the logical and best place to put it. When holographic wills have been contested in California courts for being signed but not at the end, the courts have looked at the entire document to see if it shows itself to be intended as a will. In one case, the testator wrote her name at the top of the document and added it was her last will and testament. This satisfied the court the handwritten document was her holographic will even though she did not put her signature at the end.

Because a holographic will does not require witnesses, and if none are available or you do not want any, you can at least recite that you are of sound mind and understand your purpose. Coherent writing and a statement that you understand the place and components of your property arguably evidence soundness of mind. Courts will assume testators to be of sound mind unless challengers are able to present evidence refuting it. Courts in California are inclined to try to perceive and enforce the wishes of the testator rather than not.

In this regard, California courts have considered and overlooked certain technical issues with holographic wills. For example, as long as the date is written, the court might overlook an inadvertent error if it is not critical to the will's meaning. In one of these cases, the testator had incorrectly written a portion of the date when writing out the will. In a California holographic will case called In re Estate of Wilkinson, in 1931, the testator wrote "nine hundred twenty-eight" instead of "nineteen hundred twenty-eight" in the date of the will. Because a third essential element of a valid will is that it be dated, a dissatisfied heir challenged it. The court accepted this single error as meaningless in upholding the will, stated that it was "legally sufficient," and noted the will still set forth clearly "a day, a month, a decade, and the particular year of the decade on which it purports to have been executed. Consequently the apparent inadvertence in erroneously designating the century cannot be said to destroy the effect of the instrument as a will... the designation of the century may be omitted entirely, provided the decade and the particular year of the decade be stated."

This is not to say a person can be careless. Be as complete as possible in all cases. The case of In re Wilkinson tied up the courts over the validity of a will for quite some time pondering the legitimacy of the word "nine," versus the word "nineteen." Had the testator been more careful in writing out the will, all that time and expense would have been avoided.

Holographic wills have also been ruled to be legal when written on various types of substances. The testator should choose a high-quality paper and an ink that can reasonably withstand the rigor of time, then store the will in a safe place. Other quixotic things at hand have been used, such as shirts, wood planks, napkins, cardboard, paper scraps, and melon rinds. These will work if the controlling rules of testator's own handwriting, legibility, date, signature, soundness of mind, and intent to be a will are satisfied. It is said Leo Tolstoy, the famous Russian writer, wrote out his last will and testament on a tree stump.

Unless decent pen and paper are not available in exigent circumstances, your last will and testament is not the place to express humor and eccentricity. Avoid humor if your intent to make a valid and lasting will is serious and if you do not wish your mental capacity in writing it to be questioned out of context. If a shirt, a plank, or napkin is all that is available and time is of the essence, of course, that is a different situation. You might say in the will, "this is all I have to write on."

Such exigent circumstances can be dramatically proved and are self-explanatory in some circumstances where holographic wills have been honored. Many such examples have occurred in heartrending situations on battlefields where the documents, often on bits of paper and even on helmets, survived the chaos and destruction.

One famous will was written in Saskatchewan, Canada, in 1948. A farmer named Cecil George Harris, who had become trapped under his tractor wheel for 10 hours, carved his will into the tractor's fender with his pocketknife. It read, "In case I die in this mess I leave all to the wife. Cecil Geo. Harris." Though rescued by neighbors eventually, Mr. Harris died two days later of his injuries. The fender was removed from the tractor and filed with the court for probate. The court accepted it as his valid will. The fender and Mr. Harris' knife with which he carved his will are on display in the law library at the University of Saskatchewan College of Law after having resided for many years in the courthouse.

Not only were Mr. Harris' exigent circumstances self-explanatory, he had the incredible presence of mind to make it clear by referring to "this mess" in transcribing his simple will. Further, there were witnesses to his circumstances upon his rescue.

Fill-in form will

The second type of will permitted in California is the completion of a filled in commercial form. This can be a printed and handwritten document, but it is not a holographic will. It must follow the requirements of a printed will, which means the testator must sign it or have it signed by some other person in the testator's name in the testator's presence and by the testator's direction or "by a conservator pursuant to a court order to make a will under Section 2580" of the California Probate Code. The CPC further requires the will "shall be witnessed by being signed by at least two persons each of whom (1) being present at the same time, witnessed either the signing of the will or the testator's acknowledgment of the signature or of the will and (2) understand that the instrument they sign is the testator's will."

A form will can be ordered by sending $2 and a self-addressed postage-paid business envelope to Wills, State Bar of California, Box 411, San Francisco, CA 94101.

In California, a conservator is someone appointed by a court under the CPC to handle the affairs of someone who is unable to handle his or her own affairs, or is incompetent, to avoid the person being subjected to coercion or undue influence or disadvantage. A person might request a conservator voluntarily or a conservator might be declared involuntarily by the court on the basis of clear and convincing evidence. This is a high standard that is met with strong evidence of the person's own actions and medical or psychological testimony. A person who is placed under the care of a conservator is legally unable to make a will.

In certain cases, a conservator might be appointed over the estate or property of a person who is missing and cannot be found to conserve the person's assets. This is different from management of an estate of a person who is deceased. A person who is missing cannot be declared dead immediately, so the person's will, even if there is one, cannot be considered. A missing person can be legally declared dead in California after a minimum of seven years. After that time, an application can be made to the court for a declaration of death. When death is declared, the person's will, if there is one, can be probated.

Witnesses

Witnesses are a legal requirement for wills other than holographic to be valid. Their necessity is highlighted especially in will contest actions. They could be called upon to testify to the appearance of the testator as to soundness of mind or the fact the testator signed the will him or herself in the witnesses' presence or affirmed his or signature in their presence.

CPC 6112 states that a witness must be "generally competent to be a witness." California Evidence Code 700 tells us that: "Except as otherwise provided by statute, every person, irrespective of age, is qualified to be a witness and no person is disqualified to testify to any matter." California Evidence Code 710 recognizes some limitations in persons under age 10 and the mentally impaired, however. As a general rule, it is good advice for witnesses to wills to be adults California recognizes, for most purposes, to be either age 18, emancipated, married, or a member of the Armed Forces.

The CPC places an additional limitation on witnesses to wills. Any person who benefits from the will in any manner is considered an interested person in that will. A person who benefits from the will is one who receives a bequest of money or property under it. If an interested person is one of the two requisite witnesses, the will fails to be validly executed because coercion will be presumed as a matter of law.

Your California will must be witnessed by two competent persons, preferably adults, who understand they are witnessing your signature on your last will and testament and are not named as any sort of beneficiary in the will. It is acceptable for a person named as only a fiduciary of the will to also be a witness. A fiduciary is one who is named to administer the will. Although the statute allows a fiduciary to be a witness without presuming coercion, it is still a risk. Someone who wishes to challenge the will might argue the fiduciary had something to gain whether fees for administration of the will or even something intangible, such as power. The best approach is to have witnesses who are not named in the will in any respect at all. In some situations, this might be inconvenient, but it is not difficult. Attorneys helping with will preparation can assist with provision of competent disinterested witnesses who will satisfy the statutory requirements.

You can sign the will and then have the witnesses come in later and attest your signature, but you must be present, call them both in at the same time, show them your signature, tell the witnesses the document is your last will and testament that has your own valid signature on it, and ask them to witness it by signing as witnesses. The better approach is to actually do the signing in their presence and then have each sign as witness to your signature.

It is not required that either witness be a notary public, but they can be, or you can add a notary as a third witness. Note that many California form wills have spaces for three witnesses although the statute requires a minimum of two. Witnesses should include under their signature their legible printed name, address, and telephone number. If the will is contested in the future when you are no longer able to explain what happened, the witnesses might be called upon to confirm he or she really signed as witness to the will, the other witness was there at the same time, and any other information he or she might recall about the circumstances of the will's execution.

Witnesses are important for typed and printed wills for the obvious reason that anyone can print or type a document and try to forge a name on it. It has been done more times in history than can be counted. Holographic wills are an exception because it is more difficult to forge an entire document in a testator's own handwriting than it is a single signature.

One lawyer was called out late at night by a client's son who asked him to come to the house because the client, the boy's mother, was ill and wanted the lawyer to witness her signing her new will and take it into his custody. "Couldn't this wait until morning?" the lawyer asked. "She insists it has to be you," said the son, "and I'm not sure she will last through the night." The lawyer, having served the client for many years, went to the house and was ushered into the woman's bedroom where he found her propped on her pillows, a document before her on the bed, and a pen in her hand.

The son said to him, "Mother is having trouble speaking now, but I will help her sign the will, and we can both witness it." The son took the mother's hand and started to guide it on the paper. "Wait a moment," said the lawyer, and he spoke to his client, who did not answer. He stepped closer and reached for her wrist. The son attempted to interfere, but the lawyer pushed him away and sought a pulse. As you have now guessed, the mother had already passed away. The son was attempting to get the new will signed posthumously and hoped the lawyer would either be fooled or go along with it. Of course, the son could not have been a valid witness in California because he was named in the purported will. Whatever the mother might have intended about the new will, she died before signing it and having it properly witnessed.

International Wills

CPC 6380-6390, California's codification of the Uniform International Wills Act, recognizes wills made in foreign countries, but they are subject to certain formalities of certification. The testator can have someone write the will on his behalf or write the will himself and sign it at the end in any language. If it is comprises more than one page, he or she must sign each page. According to California law, the testator must make these signatures in the presence of two witnesses plus an authorized person who is able to fill out the following Certificate. Such authorized person must be a lawyer in good standing of the California Bar or a member of the U.S. diplomatic or consular service that is empowered by U.S. law to certify international wills. The completed Certificate must be attached to the will. As with other types of wills, the testator can also attest his previously signed will before two witnesses and the authorized person. Additionally, if the testator is physically unable to sign, he or she can verbally certify this disability to the witnesses and authorized person. The authorized person will place a notation on the will, the witnesses will attest to it, and the Certificate affixed. One of the witnesses will place the testator's name as a signature on the will at the testator's direction. Notation will explain all of this on the will.

"CERTIFICATE

(Convention of October 26, 1973)

1. I, _____,
(name, address, and capacity)
a person authorized to act in connection with international wills,

2. certify that on _____ at _____
(date)   (place)

3. _____
(testator) (name, address, date and place of birth)
in my presence and that of the witnesses

4. (a) _____
(name, address, date and place of birth)

  (b) _____
(name, address, date and place of birth)

has declared that the attached document is his will and that he knows the contents thereof.

5. I furthermore certify that:

6. (a) in my presence and in that of the witnesses

    (1) the testator has signed the will or has acknowledged his signature previously affixed.

(2) following a declaration of the testator stating that he was unable to sign his will for the following reason _____, I have mentioned this declaration on the will,* and the signature has been affixed by_____

_____

(name and address)*

7. (b) the witnesses and I have signed the will;

8. (c) each page of the will has been signed by _____ and numbered;*

9. (d) I have satisfied myself as to the identity of the testator and of the witnesses as designated above;

10. (e) the witnesses met the conditions requisite to act as such according to the law under which I am acting;

11. (f) the testator has requested me to include the following statement concerning the safekeeping of his will:*

_____

12. PLACE OF EXECUTION

13. DATE

14. SIGNATURE and, if necessary, SEAL_____

*to be completed if appropriate"

Traditionally prepared printed will

The fourth type of California will is the traditional printed or typed will that is most often prepared by or with the assistance of an attorney for the testator and is signed and witnessed in the same manner as for the commercial form. Without the attestation of the testator and the signature of the witnesses as prescribed by California statute, the document will not be a valid will. It doesn't matter how professionally and meticulously prepared it is otherwise.

Changing Your Will – Codicils

You have made your will, and it is done. But along comes something new. Another child is born. New property is acquired, or property is sold. A divorce or marriage occurs. A death happens, or a loss occurs. Life changes. Whatever the reason, you decide you want to change change one provision or part of your will, or you just want to add something to it without changing the whole thing. A codicil is an addition you can write and attach to or put with your existing will. You can do it in California by the holographic method: write it by hand, sign it, date it, and designate it as a codicil to your will. If it is not holographically prepared, the codicil must meet the same witness requirement as the full will. If there are multiple codicils and they contradict each other, the most recently signed and dated codicil will be the provision that is considered valid.

Where to Keep Your Will

Keep your will in a safe place where it can also be found quickly after your death. Many people deposit their will with the attorney who helped them draft it. This is not a bad practice, especially if the attorney or his or her firm is the legal fiduciary you want to help with the probate of your will. You could also keep the will in a home safe that is fireproof or with the person you have named as your executor or executrix of the will.

In some states, it is not a good idea to keep your will in a bank safety deposit box, especially if you are the only person who has access to the box. Upon your death, access to this box will be restricted until estate papers are filed with the probate court and a fiduciary is appointed, which would be a difficult process if your will is sequestered and unavailable in that box. Even when another person has shared access to the box, the access might still be restricted. In California, this is not such an impediment; a fairly simple procedure grants access to a decedent's safety deposit box for the purpose of determining whether a will exists and obtaining the will for filing with the probate court. CPC 331 authorizes the bank to permit a person with the key to your box to have access as long as the person has proper identification and a copy of the death certificate. The bank will keep a record of the transaction. An impediment to this might arise if a dispute over who should have access is brought to the bank's attention.

Beneficiaries, Debts, and Entitlements

California permits you to distribute your property in any way you wish, but if you are married at the time of your death, your will is subject to examination of how you made provision for your spouse. California is a community property state. At the time of death of a married person, as a matter of law, one-half of the decedent's community property belongs to the surviving spouse. Unless the surviving spouse has waived all rights to inherit with full disclosure and on advice of independent legal counsel, a will's attempt to cut out the rights of a surviving spouse will fail. The court will reform the will to include the rights of the surviving spouse. Whatever property is devised will be reduced by half in favor of the surviving spouse if the will does not properly take community property into account. The remaining half will be dispersed according to the will to the extent possible. California law does provide that former spouses do not have rights to make a claim unless the testator has specifically provided for the spouse after divorce.

Children of the decedent can also make claims against a will that does not mention them. California law permits a child born or adopted after a will was made to take against the will in the same proportion the child would have been entitled by law if there had been no will at all. The same is true for a child who turns up alive who was presumed dead during the testator's lifetime or at the time the will was prepared. If a person does not wish to leave property to a child, the best approach is to name the child specifically and then state that the child cannot inherit. This rule has given rise to such unpleasant will provisions as leaving one dollar to a named offspring or excluding unknown children or future offspring not yet born from inheriting. The purpose of these provisions is to make clear the intent of the testator.

Another approach California law recognizes is to provide for the child in some way during the testator's lifetime outside the will. It is still recommended to make note of this in the text of the will so the reason substantive inheritance for that child is omitted is clear. The more explicit you can be, the more likely your wishes will be followed. They will be subject, of course, to any restrictions California law imposes.

As noted above, only legally defined "persons" can inherit as beneficiaries in a will. If you want to leave your money to your cat, you will need to first set up a trust for the animal because animals are not listed as a person who can receive property outright. California's pet trust statute is the advisable means to provide for a domestic animal.

Directions in wills that are illegal will not be carried out as a matter of law. Some directions that appear legal might also not be performed even when tied to wealthy bequests. For example, the last will and testament of Mary Murphy, a San Francisco widow who died in 1979, ordered the euthanization of her dog, Sido. It also left $200,000 to Pets, Unlimited, the animal shelter from which she had obtained Sido. She feared the dog would be lonely when she died. Thus, the testator viewed the dog's euthanization to be a kindness to ensure the dog would not fall on hard times or be unhappy.

The Society for Protection of Cruelty to Animals (SPCA) and Pets, Unlimited challenged the will's euthanization provision on behalf of Sido; it became a news story. Many people, including school children, offered homes for Sido and wrote to the court to spare Sido. Before the probate court could decide whether to honor the wishes of the testator in deciding Sido's fate, then-Governor Jerry Brown signed into law special legislation that placed Sido in the sole custody and control of Pets, Unlimited, which had vowed to keep her alive and happy. As a result, the probate court ruled the will's provision for euthanization would not be honored. Mrs. Murphy's wishes for the fate of her dog as written in her will had become illegal by statute. Sido became a California celebrity and was assured of a lifetime of honor and care for her remaining years.

Bequests to Minors

Under CPC 3900-3925, money and property of any significant value left to children under 18 will be controlled by California's Uniform Transfers to Minors Act. If you do not name a specific person to be the custodian of the property for the child until the child reaches 18, the child's "personal representative," who is the child's parent or guardian, will be the custodian of your bequest unless the court names a different person. You can also arrange in your will for property to be held in trust for a child until a later age. For this type of arrangement, you do not want to leave the details to chance. Hire a California lawyer to assist you in drafting these provisions to ensure your wishes are carried out in the way you intend. Depending on your circumstances, timing, and the type of property or extent of wealth involved, you might be better advised to create a trust for a minor during your lifetime or a pour-over testamentary trust. By setting up the trust yourself, you exercise better control over the administration of the bequest.

Intestate in California

Probate law does not permit a vacuum. If a person dies without a valid will, California law determines how to divide the person's possessions. At least half will go to the surviving spouse. Of the remaining estate, the surviving spouse will get that, too, if the decedent has no surviving children, parents, or siblings. If there is a surviving child or parents or siblings, depending on the relationship of the survivors to the decedent and the number of survivors, the estate will be divided among them as prescribed by statute. If there are no spouse and children, other blood relatives come into line by statute. The court will not take into consideration anything else, such as charities, nonrelatives, friends, or relations who might have been important to the decedent, because California law does not recognize such considerations.

Death Taxes

When making out your will and planning your estate, be sure to consult with your attorney and tax planner about the tax impact on your estate. This also will vary from state to state. There is no inheritance tax in California, and the estate tax was linked to the federal estate tax scheme. This complex area should be explored with a specialist to properly plan ahead for the tax ramifications of sizable estates. Lack of such planning will be costly because a sizeable portion of the estate can be lost to taxes and costs of administering it in the future.

How Your Will Might be Challenged

By now, you have an idea of the ways in which someone might challenge your will, or parts of it, if you have not closed the loopholes when you prepared it. The ways such challenges most often arise are:

1. The handwritten document filed with the court is not a valid holographic will because one or more of the following is missing: proper

date; signature; words indicating it is meant to be your last will and testament; and substantive parts of it are not in your handwriting.

2. It is not a holographic will and, in addition to any of the above indicia of a will being missing, it is not simultaneously witnessed by at least two competent witnesses.

3. You were not of sound mind when you wrote it.

4. Some or all of the will does not comply with California law.

5. Someone appears who claims to be your biological offspring but who is not mentioned in the will.

6. Someone appears who claims to be your lawful spouse but who is not mentioned in the will.

7. Someone comes forward with a new will or codicil of a newer date.

8. The will is claimed to be a forgery or fraud.

9. Someone claims you were under coercion.

10. One or more of the witnesses is an "interested party."

11. Community property is not accounted for in the will.

12. Arguments arise over ademption or abatement that is not addressed in the will.

If the will first presented to the probate court meets all the basic legal requirements — original, dated, intent to be a will demonstrated, disposes of property contained within, signed, and properly witnessed — the court will presume the will to be valid until proved otherwise. The challenger can file another will or codicil for the court to consider and evaluate or can challenge the will itself, but the challenger must present evidence.

Perhaps the easiest challenge to a will is producing a more recent one that exhibits all the legal requirements. When two wills are brought into question, determining which will is true often rests on the testimony of witnesses and sometimes a handwriting expert. The one with the most recent date will be the controlling will. When you make a new will, you automatically revoke all prior wills. When you make a codicil to an existing will, you only revoke a provision of the will that you are changing, not the entire will, because you are not making a new will when you prepare a codicil.

You can look ahead to potential challenges and prepare your will to prevent those challenges from affecting your wishes. Use the assistance of counsel to ensure it expresses your intent and meets the statutory requirements of a will.

A Different Type of Will – Your Living Will in California

A living will is not about dispersing your property and stating your final wishes at the time of your death. It is about having control over your body if an accident or illness puts you in a medical situation in which it is difficult or impossible for you to speak for yourself. With a living will, a person can put in writing he or she does not wish to be placed on life support systems if terminally ill or in a coma. The living will concept does not have the teeth of enforcement in all states. In California it does in the form of an Advance Health Care Directive (AHCD).

The California AHCD law actually gives a person more power than the traditional living will concept because it allows a person to state his or her wishes in any health care situation in which he or she cannot speak, not just in the coma or terminally ill situation. The California Probate Code provides a sample form for the AHCD as follows:

"ADVANCE HEALTH CARE DIRECTIVE FORM
CALIFORNIA PROBATE CODE SECTION 4700-4701

4700. The form provided in Section 4701 may, but need not, be used to create an advance health care directive. The other sections of this division govern the effect of the form or any other writing used to create an advance health care directive. An individual may complete or modify all or any part of the form in Section 4701.

4701. The statutory advance health care directive form is as follows:

ADVANCE HEALTH CARE DIRECTIVE
(California Probate Code Section 4701)

Explanation

You have the right to give instructions about your own health care. You also have the right to name someone else to make health care decisions for you. This form lets you do either or both of these things. It also lets you express your wishes regarding donation of organs and the designation of your primary physician. If you use this form, you may complete or modify all or any part of it. You are free to use a different form.

Part 1 of this form is a power of attorney for health care. Part 1 lets you name another individual as agent to make health care decisions for you if you become incapable of making your own decisions or if you want someone else to make those decisions for you now even though you are still capable. You may also name an alternate agent to act for you if your first choice is not willing, able, or reasonably available to make decisions for you. (Your agent may not be an operator or employee of a community care facility or a residential care facility where you are receiving care, or your supervising health care provider or employee of the health care institution where you are receiving care, unless your agent is related to you or is a coworker.)

Unless the form you sign limits the authority of your agent, your agent may make all health care decisions for you. This form has a place for you to limit the authority of your agent. You need not limit the authority of your agent if you wish to rely on your agent for all health care decisions that may have to be made. If you choose not to limit the authority of your agent, your agent will have the right to:

(a) Consent or refuse consent to any care, treatment, service, or procedure to maintain, diagnose, or otherwise affect a physical or mental condition.

(b) Select or discharge health care providers and institutions.

(c) Approve or disapprove diagnostic tests, surgical procedures, and programs of medication.

(d) Direct the provision, withholding, or withdrawal of artificial nutrition and hydration and all other forms of health care, including cardiopulmonary resuscitation.

(e) Make anatomical gifts, authorize an autopsy, and direct disposition of remains.

Part 2 of this form lets you give specific instructions about any aspect of your health care, whether or not you appoint an agent. Choices are provided for you to express your wishes regarding the provision, withholding, or withdrawal of treatment to keep you alive, as well as the provision of pain relief. Space is also provided for you to add to the choices you have made or for you to write out any additional wishes. If you are satisfied to allow your agent to determine what is best for you in making end-of-life decisions, you need not fill out Part 2 of this form.

Part 3 of this form lets you express an intention to donate your bodily organs and tissues following your death.

Part 4 of this form lets you designate a physician to have primary responsibility for your health care.

After completing this form, sign and date the form at the end.

The form must be signed by two qualified witnesses or acknowledged before a notary public. Give a copy of the signed and completed form to your physician, to any other health care providers you may have, to any health care institution at which you are receiving care, and to any health care agents you have named. You should talk to the person you have named as agent to make sure that he or she understands your wishes and is willing to take the responsibility.

You have the right to revoke this advance health care directive or replace this form at any time.

* * * * * * * * * * * * * * * * * *

PART 1
POWER OF ATTORNEY FOR HEALTH CARE

(1.1) DESIGNATION OF AGENT: I designate the following individual as my agent to make health care decisions for me:

_____

(name of individual you choose as agent)

_____

(address) (city) (state) (ZIP Code)

_____

(home phone) (work phone)

OPTIONAL: If I revoke my agent's authority or if my agent is not willing, able, or reasonably available to make a health care decision for me, I designate as my first alternate agent:

_____

(name of individual you choose as first alternate agent)

_____

(address) (city) (state) (ZIP Code)

_____

(home phone) (work phone)

OPTIONAL: If I revoke the authority of my agent and first alternate agent or if neither is willing, able, or reasonably available to make a health care decision for me, I designate as my second alternate agent:

_____

(name of individual you choose as second alternate agent)

_____

(address) (city) (state) (ZIP Code)

_____

(home phone) (work phone)

(1.2) AGENT'S AUTHORITY: My agent is authorized to make all health care decisions for me, including decisions to provide, withhold, or withdraw artificial nutrition and hydration and all other forms of health care to keep me alive, except as I state here:

_____

_____

_____

(Add additional sheets if needed.)

(1.3) WHEN AGENT'S AUTHORITY BECOMES EFFECTIVE: My agent's authority becomes effective when my primary physician determines that I am unable to make my own health care decisions unless I mark the following box.

If I mark this box ( ), my agent's authority to make health care decisions for me takes effect immediately.

(1.4) AGENT'S OBLIGATION: My agent shall make health care decisions for me in accordance with this power of attorney for health care, any instructions I give in Part 2 of this form, and my other wishes to the extent known to my agent. To the extent my wishes are unknown, my agent shall make health care decisions for me in accordance with what my agent determines to be in my best interest. In determining my best interest, my agent shall consider my personal values to the extent known to my agent.

(1.5) AGENT'S POSTDEATH AUTHORITY: My agent is authorized to make anatomical gifts, authorize an autopsy, and direct disposition of my remains, except as I state here or in Part 3 of this form:

_____

_____

_____

(Add additional sheets if needed.)

(1.6) NOMINATION OF CONSERVATOR: If a conservator of my person needs to be appointed for me by a court, I nominate the agent designated in this form. If that agent is not willing, able, or reasonably available to act as conservator, I nominate the alternate agents whom I have named, in the order designated.

PART 2
INSTRUCTIONS FOR HEALTH CARE

If you fill out this part of the form, you may strike any wording you do not want.

(2.1) END-OF-LIFE DECISIONS: I direct that my health care providers and others involved in my care provide, withhold, or withdraw treatment in accordance with the choice I have marked below:

|_| (a) Choice Not To Prolong Life. I do not want my life to be prolonged if (1) I have an incurable and irreversible condition that will result in my death within a relatively short time, (2) I become unconscious and, to a reasonable degree of medical certainty, I will not regain consciousness, or (3) the likely risks and burdens of treatment would outweigh the expected benefits,

OR

|_| (b) Choice To Prolong Life. I want my life to be prolonged as long as possible within the limits of generally accepted health care standards.

(2.2) RELIEF FROM PAIN: Except as I state in the following space, I direct that treatment for alleviation of pain or discomfort be provided at all times, even if it hastens my death:

_____

_____

_____

(Add additional sheets if needed.)

(2.3) OTHER WISHES: (If you do not agree with any of the optional choices above and wish to write your own, or if you wish to add to the instructions you have given above, you may do so here.)

I direct that:

_____

_____

(Add additional sheets if needed.)

PART 3
DONATION OF ORGANS AT DEATH (OPTIONAL)

(3.1) Upon my death (mark applicable box):

|_| (a) I give any needed organs, tissues, or parts, OR

|_| (b) I give the following organs, tissues, or parts only.

_____

(c) My gift is for the following purposes (strike any of the following you do not want):
(1) Transplant   (2) Therapy
(3) Research   (4) Education

PART 4
PRIMARY PHYSICIAN (OPTIONAL)

(4.1) I designate the following physician as my primary physician:

_____

(name of physician)

_____

(address) (city) (state) (ZIP Code)

_____

(phone)

OPTIONAL: If the physician I have designated above is not willing, able, or reasonably available to act as my primary physician, I designate the following physician as my primary physician:

_____

(name of physician)

_____

(address) (city) (state) (ZIP Code)

_____

(phone)

＊＊＊＊＊＊＊＊＊＊＊＊＊＊＊＊＊

PART 5

(5.1) EFFECT OF COPY: A copy of this form has the same effect as the original.

(5.2) SIGNATURE: Sign and date the form here:

_____   _____

(date)   (sign your name)

_____   _____

(address)   (print your name)

_____   _____

(city)   (state)

(5.3) STATEMENT OF WITNESSES: I declare under penalty of perjury under the laws of California (1) that the individual who signed or acknowledged this advance health care directive is personally known to me, or that the individual's identity was proven to me by convincing evidence (2) that the individual signed or acknowledged this advance directive in my presence, (3) that the individual appears to be of sound mind and under no duress, fraud, or undue influence, (4) that I am not a person appointed as agent by this advance directive, and (5) that I am not the individual's health care provider, an employee of the individual's health care provider, the operator of a community care facility, an employee of an operator of a of a community care facility, the operator of a residential care facility for the elderly, nor an employee of an operator of a residential care facility for the elderly.

First witness	Second witness
(print name)	(print name)
(address)	(address)
(city) (state)	(city) (state)
(signature of witness)	(signature of witness)
(date)	(date)

(5.4) ADDITIONAL STATEMENT OF WITNESSES: At least one of the above witnesses must also sign the following declaration: I further declare under penalty of perjury under the laws of California that I am not related to the individual executing this advance health care directive by blood, marriage, or adoption, and to the best of my knowledge, I am not entitled to any part of the individual's estate upon his or her death under a will now existing or by operation of law.

(signature of witness)	(signature of witness)

PART 6
SPECIAL WITNESS REQUIREMENT

(6.1) The following statement is required only if you are a patient in a skilled nursing facility--a health care facility that provides the following basic services: skilled nursing care and supportive care to patients whose primary need is for availability of skilled nursing care on an extended basis. The patient advocate or ombudsman must sign the following statement:

STATEMENT OF PATIENT ADVOCATE OR OMBUDSMAN

I declare under penalty of perjury under the laws of California that I am a patient advocate or ombudsman as designated by the State Department of Aging and that I am serving as a witness as required by Section 4675 of the Probate Code.

_____   _____
(date)   (sign your name)

_____   _____
(address)   (print your name)

_____   _____
(city)   (state)

October 2006"

An excellent packet for personal planning under the AHCD is provided by the National Hospice and Palliative Care Organization at **www.caring-info.org/files/public/ad/California.pdf**.

Something most people with executed living wills, or even the more comprehensive AHCD, do not realize is these documents will not prevent the administration of CPR in emergency situations unless a separate order is in place that is somehow able to be communicated to emergency responders. Typically this kind of order is not going to be issued or followed unless a person is already in such a debilitative, poor state of health that such measures are unlikely to be successful under any circumstances. It is the DNR (do not resuscitate) order and other AHCD directives that will take over later after emergency measures are past. If you are certain about the instructions you want implemented in every possible medical scenario, it is important you collaborate with medical personnel, your lawyer, and your family to ensure your instructions are followed.

As these materials demonstrate, California is both progressive and particular in the area of estate planning. Because California is a community property state with specific statutes covering a variety of estate situations, residents should know and understand what they need to do to best prepare for their wishes to be followed.

Santa Monica Harbour, California, USA

CHAPTER 12

Keeping it Current

You have a will. All your trust documents are properly executed. Your brother has agreed to be your trustee, and your sister is his backup. Your cousin is your executor, with your aunt as backup. All guardians are on board. All your beneficiaries are alive and accounted for. Insurance policies are up-to-date. You have a living will and organ donation form in the hands of your doctor. All powers-of-attorney are ready, and your retirement is fully funded. But putting together a comprehensive estate plan is just the first step. The good news is that the final step is less time-consuming.

The final step is to review your plan once a year or whenever a significant change will affect your plan or beneficiaries. If you schedule a review when you change the batteries in your smoke detectors on the first day of spring or at the end of summer, you will have time to implement any updates that will take advantage of tax law changes before the end of the fiscal year. The regular discipline means you will be able to take care of small changes quickly instead of having to go through the arduous process of making many changes all at one time.

After the volume of work that went into this plan, it might seem a yearly review is quick and easy, or it might seem too frequent for those who wish to wash their hands of the whole business. Your perspective is relative, so following the advice of those who know is a good idea. Most estate-planning professionals will tell you making many small changes throughout the year could get expensive and complicated. A decision made in the midst of a difficult experience, such as eliminating a beneficiary from your estate, could result in additional necessary changes that will cost more time and stamina than you might have available. Change your mind again later, and the process starts all over.

The annual review sets a specific time for addressing issues that come up throughout the year. It also keeps your estate plan in the back of your mind. Just as you need to remember to change the oil in your car or the engine will blow up, you need to make changes to your estate plan or it will not work the way you want it to. Once your estate plan is in place, maintenance can be simple.

What Changes?

It is not difficult to imagine the implication of some common life changes. Marriage, divorce, death of a beneficiary, the birth of a child, or loss of your job will mean obvious changes to an estate plan: changing beneficiaries, including or removing a spouse on ownership documents, and updating your name if you legally change it. Other changes are going to require some thought and planning to make the necessary adjustments to your original plan.

Property:

- You give away or sell property specified in a will or trust.
- A natural disaster destroys or causes serious damage to a piece of real estate.
- You acquire a substantial amount of new property.
- Your home is robbed and property in your will is stolen.

Health:

- You or someone in your family is diagnosed with a life-threatening illness.
- You are hurt on the job.
- A parent becomes seriously ill and cannot afford medical care.
- The doctor gives you a clean bill of health, and you can go back to work.

Good news (with strings attached):

- Your daughter is accepted into Harvard but does not qualify for student loans.
- The adoption agency in Europe approved your five-year-old application, and you need to go pick up your son next week.
- Your trustee was transferred to Nepal with no set return date.
- Your wife received a promotion and you are moving to the West Coast, which is closer to her family.

Some of these situations could mean you need to take out a loan against your retirement savings, but others will involve the thoughtful work of choosing a new personal representative and updating the related documents. Address as they arise the immediate needs, such as naming a new trustee before heading to Europe to adopt your son, but wait on others. Figuring out how to pay for a Harvard education and the implications it will have for your estate will take some time.

Check with the members of your estate-planning team to find out which kinds of changes they think should be addressed as quickly as possible and which can wait. Establish how you will communicate these things whether by e-mail, notes to an assistant, or a signed, original letter. Few finance-related companies will accept or execute directions left in a voicemail message, but a message telling your advisor an e-mail is coming and asking her to call when it arrives will suffice.

Once you are clear about the information you need to collect, make sure you are keeping track of those pieces of information throughout the year. Consolidate and organize the information to make it easy for you and your estate-planning team to have what you need. Create a file folder, make a running list, or designate a desk in your drawer for estate-planning essentials.

Make a copy of the acceptance letter from Harvard, staple to the back a printout of the tuition and fee schedule you pulled from the website, and scribble notes to yourself for reference later. If you are going to hand over documents to your lawyer or CPA, be sure to keep a copy for your files; if his or hers gets lost or you need to discuss something over the phone, having a backup copy will make things simpler.

What Does "Maintenance" Look Like?

Your estate-planning team might be a group of two or 16 individuals in one or eight different companies. Regardless of their number, they are all likely to have an idea about how to coordinate your annual review, make changes, and handle documents. With that many people involved, the potential for disaster is only slightly limited by the fact they all have a stake in making sure your plan remains intact and up-to-date. As the person with the estate, you need to decide what is most comfortable and reasonable for you.

A simple approach makes the most sense for something new. It will get complicated all by itself, so there is no need to help that along.

Make a list of each person in your estate-planning team along with their contact information, including company name and secondary contact. Then add the elements of your estate plan for which they are responsible.

The following is an example of how this contact sheet could look.

Pat Johnson, attorney at law
(Primary contact)
Dewey, Cheatum, and Howe
1234 Jokester Lane, Suite 6789
Anywhere, CA, 55555
513-555-1234 – Office
513-555-1098 – Direct line
513-555-2345 – Fax
513-555-3456 – Mobile
513-555-4567 – Home/emergency

Gail Silver, attorney at law
(Secondary contact)
Dewey, Cheatum, and Howe
1234 Jokester Lane, Suite 6789
Anywhere, CA, 55555
513-555-1234 – Office
513-555-9876 – Direct line
513-555-2345 – Fax
513-555-8765 – Mobile
513-555-7654 – Home/emergency

*** If neither contact is available, call the main number and explain the situation. The receptionist will find an alternative contact for immediate assistance. ***

Hours: M – F 8 a.m. – 6 p.m., Sat. — by appointment, Sun. — closed
Documents: Will, living will, and organ donation documents
Stored: Dewey's document vault

Once your list is compiled, look over all the contacts and decide who would make the best point person or coordinator among the group. This person will serve as the top of the phone tree. In the case of a need or emergency, you only have one person to call who will inform the rest, so you only have to say things once. If one meeting is preferred, your point person will collect and prepare all the documents needed from each person on the team so you do not have to run all over town. The person who takes on this responsibility might charge a fee for this work, but when you are short on time, the convenience is well worth the investment.

Next, you need to choose a date for that annual review. If you only have two people with whom to meet, you could schedule back-to-back appointments on the same day and take care of your work for the year. The timing of this review will depend as much on your goals for your estate plan as it will on the space in your calendar. If taxes are a primary concern, schedule your review at a point in the year that will allow you to have enough time to review the changes and make and implement decisions to maximize your savings or minimize your payments. If trusts are a big part of your estate, the same kind of review will be needed to address any changes in trust regulations.

The likelihood of having time to do a review at the end of the year might be unrealistic because of trying to squeeze in the appointments necessary between holiday parties, shopping, visits by out-of-town family, and inclement weather in some parts of the country. But spring is a busy time, too, with breaks in school schedules, graduations, and summer vacations coming up. There are more uses of your time than you thought imaginable when it comes to setting up a review of your estate plan. Ask your advisors what they think.

Periodic updates each quarter might help define when the annual review should happen. If a new tax law is passed in February, an update from your CPA in March will give you plenty of time to reach and consider the implications before the annual review you schedule for early September. Then, the children are back in school, and the holiday rush has not yet begun. This kind of attention to your plan throughout the year will make the annual sit-down less involved.

Have your planners get in touch with you a month or two in advance of your meeting to remind you it is coming and allow you to give them some directions about documents that need to be prepared. Following are a few examples of what could be happening that would be important to pass along:

- Your daughter Elizabeth just had a baby, Jeremy Jason Wolf, so you want to create a trust just like the one you have for all the other grandchildren. He also needs to be added to your will.

- Grandma Sophie passed away unexpectedly the week after Jeremy arrived. Something needs to be done about her trust for assisted-living expenses, and you need to consider suggestions about what to do with it. She also needs to be taken out of your will and her bequests given to Grandpa George.

- Kelley dropped out of business school to pursue an arts training program. Will her education trust be able to cover her expenses even though the apprenticeship-like institution is not accredited?

You could sit down and sign the necessary documents at your review. Some of your team members might regard the review as the time to go over all that information and follow up with the document signing later. Keeping your team in the loop about what is happening in your life is important so they can manage your estate plan, but you need to make sure communication supports your estate-plan goals. An e-mail or phone call when something significant occurs might be essential. Then again, waiting might not make much difference to your plan; it could save you considerable hassle given the number of times you would have to make those contacts.

What to Go Over

You need to go over all elements of your estate plan. Until the documents and routine become familiar, it could be easy to forget some of them. The Estate Planning Coordination worksheet in Appendix A is a summary of the components of your estate plan. This might include:

Will

Living will

Organ donor form/card

Durable power of attorney

Medical power of attorney

Guardians for children

Guardians for others

Life insurance policies

Disability insurance policies

Other insurance policies

Trust: For children

Trust: For retirement

Trust: For charity _____

Trust: For charity _____

Trust: Living _____

Retirement: 401(k)/pension

You will also want to consider your executor and backup, trustees and their backups, and anything else that is people-related. The goal is to make sure your documents reflect your wishes so after you are gone, no matter when that happens, your estate is disposed of the way you want. It also helps the people you leave behind, so you need to address with your estate-planning team how to make sure those things happen.

Your Desk

Federal law requires individuals and businesses to retain documentation that supports tax returns for a specific number of years. Anyone who has had to go through an audit learns the hard way this is not merely a guideline. Estate-planning documents could be considered more important than your tax records because they are the legal record dictating the disposal of your property, and what happens to that directly affects the taxes paid by your estate and every one of your beneficiaries. Stuffing those things into a cubby of an overstuffed roll-top desk and forgetting about them is not wise. Imagine your family trying to find the name of your lawyer in such a mess.

How to organize your documents and information is a personal matter. One file folder of everything might suffice, or a separate folder for each estate-planning team member might work best. You might assign one folder per document so the history of all changes is readily accessible. Whatever method you choose, be sure to include any information your family might need to access after your death. You should include the following information:

- **Contact information:** Company name, phone number, fax, e-mail address, and any other information you use to manage these accounts

- **Payment information:** Account numbers, usual due dates, and method of payment for any bills, such as automatic deductions from your checking or savings, online bill payment via your bank, coupon book, and checks mailed

- **Debts/accounts:**

- o **Real estate:** Home mortgage, second mortgage, timeshare, vacation property, and investment property

- o **Loans:** Line of credit, signature loans, and credit cards

- o **Utilities:** Gas, electric, water, sewer, heating oil, telephone, cell phone, Internet service provider, and cable/satellite

- o **Regular payments:** Car payment, insurance, automatic deposits into savings or other accounts, magazine subscriptions, and newspaper delivery

- **Resources:**

  - o **Income:** Payroll checks, rental income, structured settlement, royalties, annuity payments, and retirement distributions

  - o **Bank accounts:** Checking, savings, and certificates of deposit (CDs)

  - o **Investments:** Money market accounts

The Essential Documents and Accounts Inventory worksheet in Appendix A will help you begin assembling this information. If you already keep individual file folders for these documents so you have a place to put the stubs from the electric company or receipts from the company that delivers your heating oil, indicate the name and location of the folder. Also note whether there is a monthly payment book or the electronic delivery of notices instead of traditional mail delivery.

For the truly meticulous, it would be a good idea to have a centralized place for the original paperwork created when an account was set up, correspondences, and any other historical documents. When an executor of an estate is contacted about an outstanding debt, having access to that kind of information could make his or her job much easier.

Unfortunately, this kind of consolidation also makes it easier for a thief or unscrupulous family member to gain access to your assets. For this reason, it is important to keep these documents in a secure location. A fire-resistant home safe or locking file cabinet will make the materials readily available to you but a greater challenge for someone else.

• *Did You Know?* •

If you want to be buried instead of cremated after you are gone, you need to let your wishes be known. A former queen of England prepared every detail of her funeral, including the conveyance of her coffin to the church and who would be invited to have a seat in a pew.

Another royal not held in high esteem at the palace died unexpectedly, so a funeral had to be prepared quickly. The good news was just such a funeral plan was ready; the bad news was mostly for the former queen who planned it — all her work was going to be used by someone else.

Most people will not need a protocol book for their final arrangements, but having things done your way will require you to make your wishes known. Planning your own funeral could seem a bit morbid, but look at it this way: You plan your birthday party, so why not plan your last party, too?

One Last Motivator: Probate and You

One big reason to make sure your estate plan is up-to-date is for avoiding probate court even though it is no longer the nightmare it used to be. The probate process is designed to settle your debts and distribute your assets when the proper legal documents are not provided.

After your death, your executor is required to file your will with the probate court in the appropriate jurisdictions. If you have homes in two different states, this means filing the will with the probate court in each state. The laws in each state might be slightly different, but the process is fairly standard. The following are general laws relating to probate:

- If a person dies without a will, an administrator — or executor — is appointed by the judge. If the person dies with a will but does not use will alternatives, such as trusts, to distribute assets to beneficiaries, the named executor guides the will through the court process.

- The court posts a notice of your death, most often in local and regional papers, to notify creditors of your death and allows for a period of four or five months for any claim to be made against the estate. Once the defined window of time is closed, no more requests for payment will be considered.

- The executor/administrator notifies all beneficiaries and creditors of the estate that the administration of the will is going forward.

- The executor/administrator collects all the assets and prepares a list or inventory. Court approval must be sought to sell any assets to pay debts or make bequests.

- The executor/administrator reviews and pays all outstanding debts.

- The executor/administrator pays all taxes.

- The executor/administrator distributes the remaining assets according to the order of the court.

If the individual dies intestate, the court will designate heirs. If there is a will and the probate process is used to settle the estate, the court can also make orders about which of the beneficiaries receives what. If a particular asset that was identified as a bequest has to be sold to pay taxes, the court might order that the beneficiary of that asset be given something else or nothing.

Circumstances that influence the probate process do arise, and how each court in various states will handle these might be different. In the case of murder, most states will not permit someone who intentionally kills a person to inherit any portion of the deceased person's estate; this includes receiving the proceeds from a life insurance policy, trust, or other arrangement.

In the case of adultery or abandonment, some intestate laws will not allow the spouse who cheated or deserted to inherit anything from the estate. The evidence needed to make the case for either situation varies. One distinction is clear in most states: A missing spouse is different from abandonment. A spouse who has not voluntarily moved out but is gone without any explanation can be declared missing. A period of years must pass before any legal action can be taken. The minimum amount of time varies by state The family can then request that a person be declared legally dead, which makes it possible to execute a will, receive insurance benefits, and proceed with other estate-related activities.

The advantage of probate court is that if you have a feuding family or just do not care what happens to your belongings when you are gone, the state will take care of it for you. If either case is true, you can save yourself the work of the annual review process. If you prefer to direct things yourself, the annual review process can prevent extensive probate involvement.

If you name a beneficiary for a trust or insurance policy and that person declines the bequest or is dead, the secondary beneficiary will inherit. If you do not have a secondary beneficiary named, the probate court will settle the matter. Any issues that you do not account for in your will, will alternatives, or other estate-distribution activities will be settled by the probate court.

Taking a few hours each year to make sure your documents are in place and up-to-date is a small investment compared to the effort those who are left behind must expend.

Identity Theft

As you collect information about all your assets and liabilities and compile important personal information, it is important to be aware of safeguarding the related documentation. Identify theft is a real, dangerous threat. A person representing him or herself as another individual is a crime that can be prevented. When you do not think like a criminal, it can be difficult to figure out what you need to do to protect yourself.

Some of the ways in which a skilled identity thief will steal your information might surprise you. The following are ways to consider:

- **Change of address:** By submitting a change-of-address card with the U.S. Postal Service (USPS), the thief will send your mail to a location where he or she can get at it without suspicion.

- **Stealing:** Taking mail out of your mailbox is a bit more risky, but it does happen. Completing and returning preapproved credit cards with a change of address is just one way your mail can be used to steal your identity. Also, someone could steal your wallet, take personal records from an employer, or offer bribes to employees who have access to sell your information.

- **Garbage diving:** This is the act of looking through trash to find bills or bank statements with account information or any personal information, such as a Social Security number, mother's maiden name, or personal identification number (PIN), that might be useful in the act of stealing someone's identity. This is not considered theft; the U.S. Supreme Court has ruled that anything left out for trash collection is in the public domain.

- **Skimming:** This is accomplished by using a special high-tech storage device that electronically grabs your account number and other personal information when a store computer is processing your credit card transaction.

- **Phishing:** A thief will pretend to represent a bank, some other financial institution, or a legitimate business in the form of an e-mail or as a pop-up window when you visit a website. These communications will ask you to verify or correct information provided and then ask for additional personal information.

Avoiding identity theft

If you want to avoid being robbed on the street, there are some common-sense things you can do. Do not walk alone in a strange neighborhood at night, and only park in brightly lit parking lots. Like these behaviors, people can do some obvious things, such as cutting up old credit cards before throwing them into the trash, that help prevent identify theft. But if you throw all the pieces into the same garbage bag, a thief can reassemble the pieces and make Internet purchases because he will have access to the security code on the back of the card.

Through the unfortunate experiences of those who have had their credit rating destroyed, among other unfortunate consequences, the methods of identity thieves are no longer a secret. There are many things you can do to avoid being robbed of your good name.

The first and most important thing is awareness. Pay attention to what you are doing with your personal information. If you are scribbling notes about the accounts you need to look up and then jot them down on a piece of paper so you can enter them into a spreadsheet, do not throw that paper into the trash. Create a pile or special trashcan for "personal info." Put anything that needs to be disposed of in that one place, such as old utility bills, bank statements from an account you closed 10 years ago, or statements from your insurance company telling you a reimbursement has been made to your primary care physician. Then, choose a method for making those documents unreadable.

Invest in a small, crosscut shredder because larger scraps of paper can be reassembled like a puzzle. Remember the news clips of federal investigators hauling out bags of shredded documents from a national corporation under investigation? If your documents are not old and dusty, call your local animal shelter and ask whether they can use shredded paper for litter boxes. It is not likely a thief is going to want to go through that much effort to go through your documents once the cats, dogs, or guinea pigs are done with them. Most shredders will also destroy credit cards. Make sure you do not mix your plastic with paper going to the shelter. If you want to be safe with your credit card bits, separate the plastic bits into several different trashcans and dispose of them at different times.

Burning paper until it is a powdery ash also works well. Some other ways to prevent identity theft are equally simple, once you have them in mind.

- Never give out personal information to a stranger over the telephone or through blind mailers. If you want to register an appliance or request more information from a company, call them. Do not fill out a postcard that asks for your e-mail address, birth date, or other personal data that can be read and copied by anyone who sees it.

- Treat your Social Security number like gold; guard it the same way you would a gold coin. Do not carry your Social Security card in your wallet or purse, and never write it on a check. Only provide it when absolutely necessary, and then only to someone you have verified as an authorized agent for the company with whom you share it.

- Passwords for any account need to be unusual. Do not use the birth dates of your children, your wedding anniversary, any portion of your Social Security number, or your telephone number. Some of that information is easy to obtain through public records requests, and it will provide open access to your accounts.

- Never communicate personal information via e-mail. If you need to get the information to someone quickly, call and leave a message in a private voicemail box or send a fax to a confidential location where the information will not be handled by many people. If e-mail is a necessary means for communicating, never send complete information in one email: send most of your Social Security number in one e-mail, and send the last four digits in a second e-mail. Follow the same advice for account numbers. Even better is to e-mail part and call with the remainder. Electronic communications should not be considered secure. They can be intercepted or read by someone other than your intended audience.

- If a delivery person says she is with USPS but is stopping by to drop off a package for her friend on her way home after changing out of her uniform, refuse the package and tell her your usual letter carrier can come back tomorrow in uniform, and you will sign for it then. If that feels like being paranoid and untrusting, that is all right. You would not give your child to a stranger, so do not give yourself either, in the form of your personal information.

Be on the lookout

First and foremost, this means to protect any official documents or written materials, such as the completed worksheets from this book, so nobody has access to them unless you grant them permission. A locking file cabinet with a limited number of keys that are not numbered is one option. Standard file cabinets, like the ones you can get from a large manufacturer, have a number written on the lock. If you lose the key, you can give them that number and a few dollars, and they will send a replacement. But they will do the same for a thief, no questions asked.

A fire-resistant safe or lockbox that you can store at home will also work. Those safes are not fireproof, so whatever is inside will not necessarily survive in any fire. Fire-resistant means what is inside will be protected for a number of hours before the safe itself gets so hot that flammable material will catch fire and disintegrate. Portable boxes can also be stolen. None of this means you should not bother with these options; it just means you should be aware of the limitations of your choices.

Other choices you have for protection are being on the lookout for unusual problems:

- You are denied credit when you think your credit rating is sound.
- Bills or other information, such as letters or warranty offers, arrive for purchases you did not make.
- Bills that come at the same time every month or related to a specific purchase do not arrive as anticipated.
- Credit cards or account statements for which you did not apply are delivered.

If any of these events happen, investigate. Along those same lines, request a copy of your credit report on a regular basis, at least once a year, and check it for unusual activity; immediately follow up on anything that is suspicious. Federal law now requires nationwide credit reporting agencies to provide one free copy of your credit report each year, upon request. Visit **www.annualcreditreport.com** or call 1-877-322-8228 and request your free report. You can also write to:

Annual Credit Report Request Service
PO Box 105281
Atlanta, GA 30348-5281

Review any statements you get about existing accounts — credit card, checking, savings, money market — and see whether there is anything out of place. If something is wrong, or some vital information is stolen, act immediately.

Close any accounts that have been set up in your name but not by you or any account of yours that has been meddled with. Report the trouble immediately to your local police by filing a police report. Prepare an ID Theft Affidavit with the Federal Trade Commission, available via **www.ftc.gov** or report it via telephone at 1-877-ID-THEFT (438-4338) or TTY 1-866-653-4261. Traditional mail is also an option:

Identity Theft Clearinghouse
Federal Trade Commission
Washington. D.C. 20580

You can also place a fraud alert on your credit report; this instructs creditors to follow specific procedures before a new account is opened in your name. They will also follow these procedures when a change of personal information is requested. Before any action is taken, you can receive a phone call that will require the verification of a combination of specific personal information that would be difficult for a thief to have all at one time. There are only a few national credit reporting companies, so calling one company will let the others know that an alert has been requested — no need for you to call all three.

Equifax: 1-800-525-6285   **TransUnion:** 1-800-680-7289
Experian: 1-800-397-3742

Identity theft is a threat that should be taken seriously. Educate yourself and your family, and you will reduce your chances of being victimized.

Additional resources:
- About identity theft:
  - Federal Trade Commission: **www.ftc.gov/idtheft**
  - Identity Theft Resource Center: **www.idtheftcenter.org**
  - Social Security Administration: **www.socialsecurity.gov/pubs/10064.pdf**
- For victims of identity theft:
  - Privacy Rights Clearinghouse: **www.privacyrights.org**
  - Office of Justice Programs, Office for Victims of Crimes (OVC): **www.ojp.usdoj.gov/ovc/help/it.htm**

CONCLUSION

Congratulations: You have an estate to plan. It turns out you do not have to be rich, famous, or pompous to have the kind of resources that make it necessary to plan for the future.

The single most important thing you can do now is to create an estate plan. Even if you have done all the exercises in this book, you know there is much more work to do. The work that is necessary to move from where you are now to the point where you are scheduling regular annual meetings with estate professionals might seem a monumental task. But the good news is that it can be done. You have enough information to ask informed questions and begin to narrow down this huge idea of estate planning into your goals, will, and trusts.

The need to create your own definitions is why you did not find sample wills, a standard trust document, or an annuity template in these pages; it is counterproductive. Trying to force your information into a prescribed form supports a cookie-cutter approach to something that is highly personal. You are the one who loses with that kind of approach. The things you want to accomplish with the results of your years of hard work are not going to be like those of your brother Ben or your sister Sally. There will always be similarities, which is why books like this exist, but they need to serve as a place to begin, not end.

Customization takes time and stirs up considerable emotion and maybe even issues you would rather not face. Take your time and get the help you need with all of it. If you set your own pace and find people with whom you are comfortable, you will avoid unnecessary frustration, upset, and expense.

This is a big commitment, but when compared to the commitments it took to get to the point where you need to consider estate planning, this is a manageable process.

Build in some fun to get yourself through the difficult things. Every time you reach a milestone, such as completing your will, treat yourself to a dinner out or spend a day lounging under a tree and reading a book. Always remind yourself of the gifts you give that cannot be delineated in writing. Your wish to make your departure less burdensome, your thoughtfulness, and your love for the people in your life are all communicated through the effort of this work.

APPENDIX A

Estate-Planning Worksheets

Your Estate in Black and White

Page 1

Name _____ Birth _____ SS# _____

Spouse _____ Birth _____ SS# _____

Primary Address _____ # of Minors _____

Child _____ Birth _____ SS# _____

Child _____ Birth _____ SS# _____

Guardian of _____ Birth _____ SS# _____

ASSETS

Real Estate: *primary residence, vacation home, land*

Address/ Description	Ownership	Mortgage(s)	Purchase Price/Year	**Current Value**

Automobile(s)

Year	Make	Model	Ownership	**Current Value**

Accounts: *checking, savings, certificate of deposit, brokerage*

Type	Beneficiary(ies)	Account #	**Current Value**

Life Insurance

Company	Insured	Beneficiary(ies)	Ownership	Face Value	**Current Value**

Retirement: *401(k), IRA, Roth IRA, Keogh, pension, profit sharing, social security*

Plan	Ownership **Current Value**	Beneficiary(ies)	**Vested Year/ Percent**

Other Financial Assets: *stocks, bond, inheritance, structured settlement, rent payments*

Type	Beneficiary(ies)	Ownership	**Current Value**

Personal Property: *boat/jet ski, jewelry, artwork, antiques, collectibles, household contents, etc.*

Type	Value	Purchase Year	**Current Value**

Page 2

ADDITIONAL ASSETS			
List all of the things that did not fit on previous page of the inventory sheet:			
Type	Value	Purchase Year	**Current Value**

$ _____

Total Assets $ _____

LIABILITIES			
First mortgage, second mortgage, line of credit, car loan, and credit card balance, for example:			
Type	Ownership	Due/Payoff Year	**Current Value**

Total Liabilities $ _____

Total Assets $ _____

Total Liabilities $ _____

Total Net Worth   = $ _____

Prioritization

This is about making choices regarding what you can do with your estate. Indicate your six key values. These are the values or qualities to which you are attracted:

1.	
2.	
3.	
4.	
5.	
6.	

Then, add the one key value to orient your life around: _____

_____

Now, list all the things you would like to accomplish with your estate planning and connect those with your highest values. If more than one value is accomplished, note that.

		Goals	Value
1.	$5k	Leave a substantial amount of money to cat shelter	Involvement
2.	$50k	Education funds for niece and nephews	Education
3.	$		
4.	$		
5.	$		
6.	$		
7.	$		
8.	$		
9.	$		
10.	$		
11.	$		

After you have completed your list of goals, place an approximate dollar value for the gift you would like to leave in the left-hand margin. Use a range if you are not sure.

Total Gifts $ _____

Who, What, How, and When

After you decide on the people and organizations to receive a bequest, take a moment to write out your list. This will be useful when you sit down with your estate-planning team to finalize the paperwork and for implementation of your estate plan. Leave any places blank if you are unsure.

Who/ relationship	What	How	When	Special Circumstances
Jeanine/niece	*$50,000 + books ($10k value)*	*Trust (bequest)*	*2008*	*Will*
Cat shelter/charity	*$5,000*	*Bequest*	*2008*	*Will*
Danny/brother	*$250,000*	*Living trust/bequest*	*2008*	*Will*

Essential Documents and Accounts Inventory

Life will go on after you die, and handling your estate will likely fall to people who are mired in grief. To make it easier to find and deal with the accounts and obligations you leave behind, consolidate as much information as possible. This worksheet is a place to begin compiling that data.

This information will also be helpful to have when you meet with your estate planner.

DEBTS
Mortgage
Company Name:
Account Number:
Contact:
Phone Number:
E-mail Address:
Payment Amount:
Usual Due Date:
Method of Payment: *(automatic deductions for checking / savings, online bill payment via bank, coupon with check)*
PIN: *(Personal identification number)*
Secret Question:
Answer:
Second Mortgage
Company Name:
Account Number:
Contact:
Phone Number:
E-mail Address:
Payment Amount:
Usual Due Date:
Method of Payment:
PIN:

Secret Question:	
Answer:	
Timeshare — Mortgage Information	
Company Name:	
Account Number:	
Contact:	
Phone Number:	
E-mail Address:	
Payment Amount:	
Usual Due Date:	
Method of Payment:	
PIN:	
Secret Question:	
Answer:	
Vacation Property — Mortgage Information	
Company Name:	
Account Number:	
Contact:	
Phone Number:	
E-mail Address:	
Payment Amount:	
Usual Due Date:	
Method of Payment:	
PIN:	
Secret Question:	
Answer:	
Loans — Home Equity	
Company Name:	
Account Number:	
Contact:	
Phone Number:	
E-mail Address:	
Payment Amount:	
Usual Due Date:	
Method of Payment:	
PIN:	
Secret Question:	
Answer:	

Loans — Line of Credit	
Company Name:	
Account Number:	
Contact:	
Phone Number:	
E-mail Address:	
Payment Amount:	
Usual Due Date:	
Method of Payment:	
PIN:	
Secret Question:	
Answer:	
Loans — Signature	
Company Name:	
Account Number:	
Contact:	
Phone Number:	
E-mail Address:	
Payment Amount:	
Usual Due Date:	
Method of Payment:	
PIN:	
Secret Question:	
Answer:	
Loans — Student / College Tuition	
Company Name:	
Account Number:	
Contact:	
Phone Number:	
E-mail Address:	
Payment Amount:	
Usual Due Date:	
Method of Payment:	
PIN:	
Secret Question:	
Answer:	

Loans — Automobile
Company Name:
Account Number:
Contact:
Phone Number:
E-mail Address:
Payment Amount:
Usual Due Date:
Method of Payment:
PIN:
Secret Question:
Answer:

Loans — Other (boat, second car, etc.)
Company Name:
Account Number:
Contact:
Phone Number:
E-mail Address:
Payment Amount:
Usual Due Date:
Method of Payment:
PIN:
Secret Question:
Answer:

Credit Card #1
Company Name:
Account Number:
Contact:
Phone Number:
E-mail Address:
Payment Amount:
Usual Due Date:
Method of Payment:
PIN:
Secret Question:
Answer:

Credit Card #2
Company Name:
Account Number:
Contact:
Phone Number:
E-mail Address:
Payment Amount:
Usual Due Date:
Method of Payment:
PIN:
Secret Question:
Answer:
Credit Card #3
Company Name:
Account Number:
Contact:
Phone Number:
E-mail Address:
Payment Amount:
Usual Due Date:
Method of Payment:
PIN:
Secret Question:
Answer:
Other — Account 1
Company Name:
Account Number:
Contact:
Phone Number:
E-mail Address:
Payment Amount:
Usual Due Date:
Method of Payment:
PIN:
Secret Question:
Answer:

Other — Account 2
Company Name:
Account Number:
Contact:
Phone Number:
E-mail Address:
Payment Amount:
Usual Due Date:
Method of Payment:
PIN:
Secret Question:
Answer:

Other — Account 3
Company Name:
Account Number:
Contact:
Phone Number:
E-mail Address:
Payment Amount:
Usual Due Date:
Method of Payment:
PIN:
Secret Question:
Answer:

LIVING EXPENSES

Gas and Electric
Company Name:
Account Number:
Contact:
Phone Number:
E-mail Address:
Payment Amount:
Usual Due Date:
Method of Payment:
PIN:
Secret Question:
Answer:

Water and Sewer (or septic)
Company Name:
Account Number:
Contact:
Phone Number:
E-mail Address:
Payment Amount:
Usual Due Date:
Method of Payment:
PIN:
Secret Question:
Answer:
Telephone
Company Name:
Account Number:
Contact:
Phone Number:
E-mail Address:
Payment Amount:
Usual Due Date:
Method of Payment:
PIN:
Secret Question:
Answer:
Heating Oil
Company Name:
Account Number:
Contact:
Phone Number:
E-mail Address:
Payment Amount:
Usual Due Date:
Method of Payment:
PIN:
Secret Question:
Answer:
Internet Service Provider (ISP)
Company Name:

Account Number:	
Contact:	
Phone Number:	
E-mail Address:	
Payment Amount:	
Usual Due Date:	
Method of Payment:	
PIN:	
Secret Question:	
Answer:	
Cable / Satellite Television Service	
Company Name:	
Account Number:	
Contact:	
Phone Number:	
E-mail Address:	
Payment Amount:	
Usual Due Date:	
Method of Payment:	
PIN:	
Secret Question:	
Answer:	
Other — Account 1	
Company Name:	
Account Number:	
Contact:	
Phone Number:	
E-mail Address:	
Payment Amount:	
Usual Due Date:	
Method of Payment:	
PIN:	
Secret Question:	
Answer:	
Other — Account 2	
Company Name:	
Account Number:	
Contact:	

Phone Number:	
E-mail Address:	
Payment Amount:	
Usual Due Date:	
Method of Payment:	
PIN:	
Secret Question:	
Answer:	
OTHER REGULAR PAYMENTS	
Insurance: Life — Policy 1	
Company Name:	
Account Number:	
Contact:	
Phone Number:	
E-mail Address:	
Payment Amount:	
Usual Due Date:	
Method of Payment:	
PIN:	
Secret Question:	
Answer:	
Insurance: Life — Policy 2	
Company Name:	
Account Number:	
Contact:	
Phone Number:	
E-mail Address:	
Payment Amount:	
Usual Due Date:	
Method of Payment:	
PIN:	
Secret Question:	
Answer:	
Insurance: Life — Disability (Long/Short-Term)	
Company Name:	
Account Number:	
Contact:	
Phone Number:	

E-mail Address:	
Payment Amount:	
Usual Due Date:	
Method of Payment:	
PIN:	
Secret Question:	
Answer:	
Insurance: Life — Homeowner's / Renter's	
Company Name:	
Account Number:	
Contact:	
Phone Number:	
E-mail Address:	
Payment Amount:	
Usual Due Date:	
Method of Payment:	
PIN:	
Secret Question:	
Answer:	
Insurance: Car — Policy 1	
Company Name:	
Account Number:	
Contact:	
Phone Number:	
E-mail Address:	
Payment Amount:	
Usual Due Date:	
Method of Payment:	
PIN:	
Secret Question:	
Answer:	
Insurance: Car — Policy 2	
Company Name:	
Account Number:	
Contact:	
Phone Number:	
E-mail Address:	
Payment Amount:	

Usual Due Date:	
Method of Payment:	
PIN:	
Secret Question:	
Answer:	
Newspaper Subscription 1	
Company Name:	
Account Number:	
Contact:	
Phone Number:	
E-mail Address:	
Payment Amount:	
Usual Due Date:	
Method of Payment:	
Newspaper Subscription 2	
Company Name:	
Account Number:	
Contact:	
Phone Number:	
E-mail Address:	
Payment Amount:	
Usual Due Date:	
Method of Payment:	
Magazine Subscription 1	
Company Name:	
Account Number:	
Contact:	
Phone Number:	
E-mail Address:	
Payment Amount:	
Usual Due Date:	
Method of Payment:	
Magazine Subscription 2	
Company Name:	
Account Number:	
Contact:	
Phone Number:	

E-mail Address:	
Payment Amount:	
Usual Due Date:	
Method of Payment:	
Magazine Subscription 3	
Company Name:	
Account Number:	
Contact:	
Phone Number:	
E-mail Address:	
Payment Amount:	
Usual Due Date:	
Method of Payment:	
Other — Account 1	
Company Name:	
Account Number:	
Contact:	
Phone Number:	
E-mail Address:	
Payment Amount:	
Usual Due Date:	
Method of Payment:	
PIN:	
Secret Question:	
Answer:	
Other — Account 2	
Company Name:	
Account Number:	
Contact:	
Phone Number:	
E-mail Address:	
Payment Amount:	
Usual Due Date:	
Method of Payment:	
PIN:	
Secret Question:	
Answer:	

INCOME

Payroll Check 1

Company Name:	
Account Number:	
Contact:	
Phone Number:	
E-mail Address:	
Check Amount:	
Pay Day/Dates:	
Method of Payment: *(check, direct deposit, cash, other)*	
Additional Important Information:	

Payroll Check 2

Company Name:	
Account Number:	
Contact:	
Phone Number:	
E-mail Address:	
Check Amount:	
Pay Day/Dates:	
Method of Payment: *(check, direct deposit, cash, other)*	
Additional Important Information:	

Structured Settlement

Company Name:	
Account Number:	
Contact:	
Phone Number:	
E-mail Address:	
Check Amount:	
Day/Dates Paid:	
Method of Payment: *(check, direct deposit, cash, other)*	
Additional Important Information:	

Royalty Payment 1
Company Name:
Account Number:
Contact:
Phone Number:
E-mail Address:
Check Amount:
Day/Dates Paid:
Method of Payment: *(check, direct deposit, cash, other)*
Additional Important Information:

Royalty Payment 2
Company Name:
Account Number:
Contact:
Phone Number:
E-mail Address:
Check Amount:
Day/Dates Paid:
Method of Payment: *(check, direct deposit, cash, other)*
Additional Important Information:

Annuity Payment 1
Company Name:
Account Number:
Contact:
Phone Number:
E-mail Address:
Check Amount:
Day/Dates Paid:
Method of Payment: *(check, direct deposit, cash, other)*
Additional Important Information:

Annuity Payment 2
Company Name:
Account Number:
Contact:
Phone Number:
E-mail Address:
Check Amount:
Day/Dates Paid:
Method of Payment: *(check, direct deposit, cash, other)*
Additional Important Information:

Retirement Distribution — Plan 1
Company Name:
Account Number:
Contact:
Phone Number:
E-mail Address:
Check Amount:
Day/Dates Paid:
Method of Payment: *(check, direct deposit, cash, other)*
Additional Important Information:

Retirement Distribution — Plan 2
Company Name:
Account Number:
Contact:
Phone Number:
E-mail Address:
Check Amount:
Day/Dates Paid:
Method of Payment: *(check, direct deposit, cash, other)*

Rental Property 1
Company Name:
Account Number:
Contact:

Phone Number:	
E-mail Address:	
Check Amount:	
Day/Dates Paid:	
Method of Payment: *(check, direct deposit, cash, other)*	
Tenant Information:	

Rental Property 2

Company Name:	
Account Number:	
Contact:	
Phone Number:	
E-mail Address:	
Check Amount:	
Day/Dates Paid:	
Method of Payment: *(check, direct deposit, cash, other)*	
Tenant Information:	

FINANCIAL RESOURCES

Checking — Account 1

Financial Institution:	
Account Number:	
Contact:	
Phone Number:	
E-mail Address:	
Balance:	
Date:	
PIN:	
Secret Question:	
Answer:	
Additional Important Information:	

Checking — Account 2

Financial Institution:	
Account Number:	

Contact:	
Phone Number:	
E-mail Address:	
Balance:	
Date:	
PIN:	
Secret Question:	
Answer:	
Additional Important Information:	
Savings — Account 1	
Financial Institution:	
Account Number:	
Contact:	
Phone Number:	
E-mail Address:	
Balance:	
Date:	
PIN:	
Secret Question:	
Answer:	
Additional Important Information:	
Savings — Account 2	
Financial Institution;	
Account Number:	
Contact:	
Phone Number:	
E-mail Address:	
Balance:	
Date:	
PIN:	
Secret Question:	
Answer:	
Additional Important Information:	

Certificate of Deposit — Account 1
Financial Institution:
Account Number:
Contact:
Phone Number:
E-mail Address:
Balance:
Date:
PIN:
Secret Question:
Answer:
Additional Important Information:

Certificate of Deposit — Account 2
Financial Institution:
Account Number:
Contact:
Phone Number:
E-mail Address:
Balance:
Date:
PIN:
Secret Question:
Answer:
Additional Important Information:

Money Market Fund — Account 1
Financial Institution:
Account Number:
Contact:
Phone Number:
E-mail Address:
Balance:
Date:
PIN:
Secret Question:
Answer:

Additional Important Information:	
Money Market Fund — Account 2	
Financial Institution:	
Account Number:	
Contact:	
Phone Number:	
E-mail Address:	
Balance:	
Date:	
PIN:	
Secret Question:	
Answer:	
Additional Important Information:	
Other — Account 1	
Financial Institution:	
Account Number:	
Contact:	
Phone Number:	
E-mail Address:	
Balance:	
Date:	
PIN:	
Secret Question:	
Answer:	
Additional Important Information:	
Other — Account 2	
Financial Institution:	
Account Number:	
Contact:	
Phone Number:	
E-mail Address:	
Balance:	
Date:	
PIN:	

Secret Question:
Answer:
Additional Important Information:

Anything that did not fit in a predetermined category: _____

_____

_____

_____

_____

Party Planning with an Unusual Twist

Whether you prefer a traditional and dignified ceremony or an occasion that is a reflection of how you lived your life, the arrangements for the last event you will attend on Earth in this lifetime can be up to you. But you need to make the necessary arrangements or direct others to do as you wish. *This is not a legally binding document; a lawyer will need to be consulted for the correct language and paperwork.*

Check all that apply (leave blank those things you do not want) and provide any details that are needed.

Your body:

☐   I want my body to be donated to medicine and used for the following purposes: _____

_____

☐   Release the final report, including all test results, to my executor/personal representative: _____

_____

☐ Conduct a postmortem examination if the following circumstances occur: _____

_____

☐ Cremate my remains. Disposal of my ashes should be conducted as follows: _____

_____

☐ I request a burial to take place in this way: _____

_____

Your service:

☐ I want a memorial service without a casket.

☐ I want a funeral without a casket.

☐ Memorial service with a casket conducted in the following manner:

    ☐ Closed
    ☐ Open
    ☐ Funeral home/mortuary: _____
    Address: _____
    Phone: _____

☐ I would like a funeral service conducted in the following manner:

    Place of worship: _____

    Address: _____

    Phone: _____

    Presiding clergy: _____

    Soloist: _____

    Hymns: _____

    _____

Musical selections: _____

_____

Musical instruments: _____

_____

Scripture, poem(s), and other materials to be included: _____

_____

_____

Other instructions: _____

_____

_____

_____

_____

Memorial gifts should be suggested for the following: _____

_____

_____

Other information: _____

_____

_____

Signed: _____ Date: _____

Estate Plan Summary Sheet

Many components can go into an estate plan, but there are some basic documents most people have. This is a brief inventory that can serve as a checklist for making sure you get the things done you need to accomplish.

Use the blank lines to add other documents, such as a prenuptial agreement, that will affect your estate plan.

Estate Plan Components	Deadline	Done On	Notes
Estate Plan Summary Sheet			
Will			
Living Will			
Organ Donor Form/Card			
Durable Power of Attorney			
Medical Power of Attorney			
Guardians for Children			
Guardians for Others			
Life Insurance Policies			
Trust: For Children			
Trust: For Retirement			
Trust: For Charity _____			
Trust: For Charity _____			
Trust: Living _____			
Retirement: 401(k)/Pension _____ _____ _____ _____			

Use the Notes sections as reminders for additional information that is needed before the next review. For example, write "Get name of Peace Center lawyer" to make sure you have a contact for the charitable trust documents that might need to get to the organization.

Annual To-Do List

Once your estate plan is complete, this list will need to be customized to include each component.

Use the blank lines to add other documents, such as a prenuptial agreement, that will affect your estate plan.

Estate Plan Pieces	Meeting Date	Changes Needed
Estate Plan Summary Sheet		
Will		
Living Will		
Organ Donor Form/Card		
Durable Power of Attorney		
Medical Power of Attorney		
Guardians for Children		
Guardians for Others		
Life Insurance Policies		
Trust: _____		
Trust: _____		
Trust: _____		
Trust: _____		
Retirement: _____		

Retirement: _____

_____

_____

_____

_____

Notes:

APPENDIX B

Glossary of Terms

401(k) Plan – Named after the IRS code number defining this kind of plan, this retirement savings plan allows contributions to be made automatically by your employer via deductions from your paycheck, pretax. This plan only applies to for-profit businesses.

403(b) Plan – This is the 401(k) equivalent for nonprofit entities and is named after the IRS code number defining this kind of retirement savings plan. It allows contributions to be made automatically by your employer via deductions from your paycheck, pretax.

A

Adeemed – The status given to a will if property is missing from your estate that is specifically named in the will.

Ademption Statute – State law governing the distribution of property in an estate if items are missing or adeemed.

Administrator – If you die without a will, the court appoints an individual, normally a spouse or child, who will serve in the same capacity as an executor. That person will handle all the estate paperwork, prepare a list of assets, deal with likely heirs, handle claims from creditors, make payments on outstanding debt, and handle other estate-related matters.

Advance Health Care Directive – California's statute allowing people to write out their wishes for removal of life support and how their health care is to be provided in any situation in which they cannot speak, not just in a terminally ill situation. California's advance health care directive exceeds the power of a traditional living will.

▶ **Annuity** – A retirement investment account that you create by contributing a specific amount of money over a predetermined period of time; there will be a fixed rate of return for a number of years.

Variable Annuity – A retirement investment account that you create by contributing a specific amount of money over a predetermined period of time; the funds are invested in the stock market, so the return depends on how well or poorly the economy does.

Antilapse – The status of a will if a beneficiary in your will dies before you do.

Antilapse Statute – State law that dictates the state will intervene if the property in a will exists, but the beneficiary is no longer alive, and no contingent beneficiary is named.

Appointment Clause – A giving clause in your will that identifies the person who will manage your estate.

Asset – Anything a person owns or is owed; this can be money, real estate, investments, or any other tangible property.

Automobile Insurance – The exchange of premiums for a guaranteed payment to cover the damage or loss of a motor vehicle. Medical and liability coverage can also be included.

B

Bargain Sale – The sale of a piece of property to a charity at a rate that is below the fair market value. The difference between the amount paid and actual value is the amount of the gift.

Beneficiary – The individual(s) or group(s) that will receive the property in a will or trust. This can be a single person (a nephew), a group of people (all grandchildren), one group (Stray Cat Rescue, Inc.), several groups (all community councils in your city), or a combination of any of these.

Beneficial Title, or Equitable Title – The right of a person or institution to take possession of or benefit from the property in a trust.

Bequest – A legacy or gift given by a person to another person or entity through a last will and testament after the giver dies.

Burial Trust – Provides the funds necessary to cover the cost of your burial (or cremation) arrangements; this can be a revocable trust, but after your death, it becomes irrevocable, and the trust cannot be used for anything else.

Bypass Trust – This trust will transfer property to someone other than your spouse, such as a child or grandchild, but will allow him or her to still benefit from the property in the trust.

C

Certified Public Accountant (CPA) – A person who has gone through professional training and meets state requirements for both education and work experience, passed a national accounting exam, and met other licensing requirements to perform the tasks of accounting such as performing audits, preparing tax returns, and giving advice to their clients — individuals or businesses — on financial matters. Accountants can also specialize in various aspects of financial estate matters such as trusts, annuities, and estate tax law. But they also serve as estate-planning specialists who can help you consider all financial decisions.

Charitable Trust – A method for giving charitable institutions gifts, including regular support on a time-release basis, that are tax-free for the donor.

Charitable Remainder Trust – Gives gifts of interest income that are paid to specific beneficiaries, such as the charity or a spouse, for a specific period of time; at the end of that time period, the charity receives whatever is left in the trust.

Charitable Lead Trust – Also known as a front trust; gives the charity a specific gift before all other beneficiaries receive anything.

Clauses – The sections in your will that organize the information in a specific order.

Coach – These trained professionals specialize in offering financial, professional, and personal guidance to help you identify and manage monetary, career, and personal goals. There are certification courses for various forms of coaching, but there are no national standards, and formal training is not required to present oneself as a coach.

Codicil – A separate legal document that adds provisions to your existing will.

Conservator – Under California law, a person who is placed in charge of an estate by the probate court on behalf of another who is a minor or otherwise deemed incompetent to handle his or her affairs; comparable to a guardian.

Cost-of-living Adjustment – Some plans have a variable that will allow for annual increases in the payments made to the employee to help cover the cost of rising prices. Not all plans have this feature.

Crummey Trust – An extremely complicated trust normally set up in conjunction with an irrevocable life insurance trust to make the payments for a life insurance policy; this is the kind of trust that requires an estate-planning attorney.

Custodian Account – This account for minor children, which can be in the form of a trust, allows you to deposit money or property in an account set up by a bank or brokerage firm. You can name yourself as the custodian, or trustee, of the account while you are alive and then name a successor to take over those responsibilities after you die.

▶ **Uniform Transfer for Minors Act (UTMA)** – This is the most current federal regulation that defines and allows an account, or trust, to be set up for minor children; if a state adopted this regulation, it served to repeal their UGMA statute.

▶ **Uniform Gift to Minors Act (UGMA)** – This is the first federal regulation that defined and allows an account, or trust, to be set up for minor children; some states still have this form of the law on their books.

D

Decedent – A person who has died.

Disability Insurance – A disability insurance policy that will make payments to you to cover living expenses and replace your lost income as a result of your inability to hold a job.

▶ **Short-term Disability** – Provides benefits for about three months; some plans go a little longer, but only for a short period of time.

▶ **Long-term Disability** – Provides benefits for years but does eventually end, frequently at age 65, when you become eligible for Social Security.

Disclaimer – A refusal of a beneficiary to accept the gift given; recognized by both federal and state authorities if given in writing by a specific deadline, typically nine months after the donor's death.

Discretionary Trust – Gives a trustee the ability to distribute income and property to a variety of beneficiaries; he or she also has the option to control the distributions to a single beneficiary as he or she decides is appropriate.

Distribution – This is the disbursement or payment of property from an account to a beneficiary; it could be in the form of a check or some other monetary payment, or the transfer of a title into the name of the beneficiary.

Distribution Provisions – Any clause that identifies to whom the income will be given and the frequency of those distributions, such as payments made every April 15 to the IRS.

DNR – Do not resuscitate: an advanced medical directive that expresses your wish to not be resuscitated or revived if you appear to have died.

Donee – The person or institution receiving a gift.

Donor – The person who gives a gift or bequest.

Dumpster Diving – A slang term used to describe the act of digging through trash to find bills, bank statements, or other documents with account information or any personal information that might be useful to an identity thief; this is not considered an act of theft because the U.S. Supreme Court ruled that anything left out for trash collection is in the public domain.

Durable Power of Attorney – Allows an authorized person to act on behalf of the grantor of that power of attorney.

Dynasty Trust – Also known as a wealth trust; can last for several generations or be set up to never end. This kind of trust helps people with a vast amount of wealth control the distribution of that money and property over a long period of time.

E

Educational Trust – This is a kind of protective trust that sets aside money specifically for education-related expenses, such as tuition or training fees, books, or supplies. These trusts include provisions to stop payments if the student drops out of school or flunks numerous classes.

Ending Clauses – These include the legalities to meet statutory requirements so that your will is legal and valid, which include (but are not limited to) your signature, date, location of the signing, and witnesses.

Estate Planning – Creating a set of instructions about what should be done with your things — money, possessions, investments, collectibles, or anything you own — before and after you die.

Estate Tax – Referred to as the "death tax" by Congress, this is the federal tax on the property in your estate after you die.

Executor – Also called a personal representative, this is the individual who handles the property you are leaving behind. If you die without a will, the court appoints an administrator, frequently a spouse or child.

Exemption – This is a specific amount of money that will not be affected by estate taxes. Federal taxes and states with an estate tax often set an amount, such as $1 million, that is tax-free, taxes are due on $1.01 million and beyond.

F

Family Consent – Also known as a health surrogate, this is a family member designated by state law who will make medical decisions for you when you cannot do it for yourself. These laws follow a specific order of kinship for who makes a decision — if you are married, your spouse, not your sister, will be your surrogate.

Family Trust – A legal arrangement that involves the transfer of property from the original owner to a family member for the purpose of holding and maintaining the property until the beneficiary takes ownership.

Fiduciary Powers Clause – A giving clause in your will that includes language giving your executor the power to serve as your executor, including any duties that go beyond the basic requirements in your state regulations.

Financial Planner – Certified Financial Planners® (CFP®), Chartered Financial Analysts (CFA), and some without initials are individuals who analyze the overall financial situation of an individual and then develop a comprehensive plan, in conjunction with the individual, that will attempt to meet his or her financial goals and objectives. Planners who are certified have followed a specific course of education or training classes, and some go on to develop expertise in specific areas such as estate or retirement planning.

Funding a Trust – The placement of property in a trust; that same property will be called "trust principal" once it is under the auspices of the trust agreement.

G

Generation-Skipping Tax Transfer (GSTT) – This is a federal tax levied on property transferred to a person one or more generations removed from the donor.

Generation-Skipping Transfer Trust – A tax-saving trust that is designed to benefit multiple generations after you are gone.

Gift Tax – A federal tax levied against any property you give to another person or institution during a fiscal year; it can be in cash or the transfer of property, such as real estate or jewelry.

Giving Clauses – Explain what property goes to which person and under what circumstances. These can be as broad or explicit as you want. Real property clauses are statements that match up property with a person. Personal property clauses are used when you want to be explicit in your instructions. A residuary clause addresses the "leftovers" in your estate that you do not single out in a clause; this clause is essential for any kind of will to make sure that anything you forget or acquire since the will was prepared can be distributed. Making one or two beneficiaries is a good idea to keep your assets out of the hands of the courts.

Grantor-Retained Trusts – These are irrevocable, non-charitable trusts, which means they are set up in a way that is similar to a charitable trust, but the beneficiary is not a charity. There are three common types:

GRAT – Grantor-retained annuity trust gives a fixed amount of money at predetermined times, often at regularly scheduled intervals.

GRIT – Grantor-retained incomes trust designates specific people to receive certain property, such as stocks or a house, but the income or use of the property stays with you until your death.

GRUT – Grantor-retained unit trust pays a specific percentage to the beneficiary.

Gross Estate – The value of all property owned by the deceased person on the date of that person's death; this is what gets taxed.

Guardian – The person legally appointed to be responsible for the needs of minor children until they reach a legal age; also, any adult who can be legally appointed to manage the affairs of an incompetent or infirmed adult of any age.

Guardianship Clause – The appointment of a guardian for minor children (under the age of 18); a successor guardian should also be named as a backup.

H

Health Care Power of Attorney – Also known as medical power of attorney, this is the designation of a person who makes medical decisions for you when you cannot do it for yourself.

Heir – The legal title of a person who inherits property from an estate that does not have a will, or is intestate; beneficiaries are those who receive an inheritance by being named in a legal document, such as a will or trust.

Holographic Will – This is a handwritten document signed by you but not witnessed by anyone else. Some states like California recognize a handwritten will as valid; others do not, so you need to check your state laws if you want to use this kind of will.

Homeowner's Insurance – The exchange of premiums for a guaranteed payment to cover the loss of a house and other personal property in the residence. Other coverage can also be included, such as personal liability.

Homestead Exemption Statute – State law that protects a family home from being sold to pay off creditors if there is not enough money in an estate to cover outstanding debt.

I

Individual Retirement Arrangement (IRA) – An investment account that you set up for yourself for retirement savings. There is a limit to the contributions you can make annually. There is a tax deduction for making these contributions every year, so technically they are tax-free contributions.

▶ **Roth IRA** – Named after its primary legislative sponsor, Senator William Roth of Delaware. Contributions to this IRA are also tax-deductible in the year they are made, and taxes are paid when the money is withdrawn. The difference here is that the interest earned while the money is invested will be tax-free if you own the Roth IRA for at least five years.

Inheritance Tax – A state tax levied on the property received by a beneficiary.

Insurance – A method of protecting valuables in the form of a policy in which premiums are paid over time to guarantee a specific payment for a specific purpose by the company accepting the premiums. Those valuables can be property, such as your home, car, or jewelry; a person; the ability to work and care for yourself; life; health care; and long-term care.

Insurance Agent – An individual who is authorized by an insurance company to represent that company when dealing with an applicant for insurance, be it a medical, disability, dental, or long-term care policy. An agent can help you with your policy purchase by assessing the kind and amount of insurance you need and can afford.

Intestate – To die without a will.

Inter vivos Trust – A trust that is set up and takes effect during your lifetime, before your death.

Irrevocable – A trust that cannot be changed, no matter what.

J

Joint Will – This is one legal document for any two people, such as you and your spouse. The problem with this kind of will is that it is irrevocable, which means it cannot be changed after one of the two parties dies. The reason is that all decisions must be made by both people. A lawyer can tell you when this kind of will is a good idea, but most suggest separate wills to avoid complications.

Joint-with-survivor Pension – When an employee dies, his or her benefits will be paid to his or her spouse for the remainder of the spouse's life. If the spouse waives that right, the employee's pension payments will be larger (no need to set aside extra money for future payments), and the pension payments end when the employee dies.

K

Keogh Plan – Pronounced "key-oh," this is a qualified retirement plan for sole proprietors and partners but can also be used by employees. The restrictions, distributions, and other details are similar to a defined contribution plan or defined benefit plan.

"Kiddie Tax" – The nickname used to describe an income tax applied to money that minors did not earn through employment, also called unearned income. The special laws passed in 1996 were created to close a loophole that allowed parents to give their children a large gift as a way to pay a lower tax on the interest earned; the child tax rate was significantly lower than the adult rate.

L

Lawyer – An individual who has completed a course of study in the law and passed a state certification exam that authorizes him or her to practice law and/ or give legal advice. Also called attorneys, these people can specialize in specific aspects of estate planning, such as wills, trusts, or probate court, or they might have a more broad focus, such as estate planning or tax law.

Legal Title – Legal position that gives the trustee ownership of the property in a trust for the duration of the trustee's responsibility.

Liability – A debt or an obligation to pay money to another person or institution.

Life Insurance – A financial arrangement in which an individual makes payments on a policy that guarantees the payment of a specific amount of money to a beneficiary upon the death of the person who is covered by the policy.

Living Trust – Created while you are still alive, this trust allows you to be the grantor, trustee, and beneficiary if you choose; this is considered a will substitute as a way to avoid probate.

Living Will – Also known as a medical directive, this is a legal document in which you spell out the decisions you have made about your medical care while you are still alive.

Long-term Care Insurance – This insurance provides payments to cover the cost of medical care. In-home nursing or nursing home fees are examples of what might be covered.

M

Marital Dedication Trust – Puts property into a trust that is exclusively for your spouse, who decides what happens to the property after your death.

Medical Insurance – Frequently referred to as health insurance by those who sell it, the insurance that covers medical costs when you are sick and trying to cure an illness, injured, pregnant, and for regular checkups.

Medicaid – State-run medical insurance plan that is supported by federal funding and provides medical benefits that are minimal for the financially needy. To qualify for this plan, you have to possess no more than a set dollar amount in property.

Medicare – A medical insurance program offered by the federal government to people who are 65 or older, certain disabled people under the age of 65, and anyone with permanent kidney failure.

▶ **Part A** of this coverage is hospital insurance and **Part B** is medical insurance. Part B now comes with a monthly premium.

Medical Power of Attorney – Also known as health care power of attorney, this is the designation of a person who makes medical decisions for you when you cannot do it for yourself.

Minor Trust – A way to give gifts to a minor that avoids the gift tax and keeps the property safe until the minor becomes an adult and can take ownership of the trust.

Marital Trust – A trust for the surviving legal spouse of the deceased.

Mutual Will – A plan for your estate that is prepared in conjunction with another person.

N

Net Worth – A person's true financial value: Assets – Liabilities = Net Worth.

Non-Charitable Trust – A trust that has a person or institution that is not a charity as the beneficiary.

Non-Statutory Living Will – A legal document in which you spell out the decisions you have made about your medical care while you are still alive that does not comply with the laws of your state. A statutory document will likely provide more protection for the physicians and nurses carrying out your wishes.

Nuncupative Will – Also called an oral will, this is a spoken will. Some states only allow this kind of will if someone is literally on their deathbed, and it only covers personal property of little or no value. Again, you need to check with your state on the laws regarding this kind of will. California does not recognize this type of will.

O

Opening Clauses – Lay out the basic information about who you are and set the stage for the clauses that follow. The introductory clause identifies you as the person who is making the will, the family statement clause introduces and identifies the family members who will be referred to later in the will, and the tax clause explains how the taxes on your estate will be paid.

Outright Charitable Gift – This is property you give to a charity and get nothing in return for; the gift can be cash or any other type of property.

Ownership – The individual(s) who hold the legal title to a piece of property; the ability to retain, sell, or give away this property depends on the number of people who hold that title, in some cases, their relationship, and any legal agreements/contracts connected to the property.

▶ **Sole Ownership** – A single person holds the title to the property.

▶ **Joint Ownership** – When any two people hold an equal share of the title to a piece of property; the most common form is spousal, or when a legally married couple has both names on a title to a piece of property.

▶ **Community Property** – A state law that views a wife and husband as equal partners and assumes a 50/50 split of ownership. California is a community property state.

▶ **Separate Property** – Things owned by one spouse that are not part of the couple's community property.

▶ **Joint Tenancy** – A group of people who hold an equal and undivided title to a piece of property.

P

Payable-on-Death (POD) – An account, like a savings account, that has a specific stipulation that the death of the original owner automatically transfers the ownership to a named beneficiary.

Pension Benefit Guarantee Corporation (PBGC) – A federal agency that can insure and therefore protect some or all of your pension, if your plan qualifies for the coverage and your company purchases the insurance.

Pension Plan – A program that is set up by an employer, including government agencies, to pay employees benefits upon retirement. Each employee has an individual account, and the employer makes a contribution to each employee's account based on the terms of the plan. There are two common types of pension plans.

▶ **Defined Benefit Plan** – A plan in which the employee will receive a specified amount of money upon retirement; the amount of the disbursement made is based on the number of years of employment.

▶ **Defined Contribution Plan** – A pension plan that sets a specific amount an employee will put into the plan (a percentage of income) and makes payments only for the amount of money contributed to the plan.

Phishing – The act of fraudulently representing an e-mail, website pop-up window, or other electronic communication as being from a bank, some other financial institution, or a legitimate business that requests the verification of personal information. These communications also request "missing" information and updates to intentionally incorrect data.

Pourover Will – This will place some property into a trust that was established while you were still alive.

Probate Court – The state-level court system that is specifically set up to handle all matters related to the distribution of a deceased person's estate; this is where a will is filed and unanswered questions about the disbursement of an estate are settled by a judge.

Profit-sharing Plan – Employees receive a portion of the profits earned by the company; the plan determines the amount that will be contributed to each employee's account.

Property – Also referred to as personal property, this comprises your possessions. This category is further divided into:

▶ **Real Property** – Any kind of real estate, such as a house, a condo, or a vacant lot.

▶ **Tangible Personal Property** – The things you can touch, such as a signed baseball, jewelry, or linen bed sheets.

▶ **Intangible Personal Property** – Checking accounts, savings accounts, money market funds, mutual funds, stocks, bonds, or retirement accounts such as a pension, an IRA, a Roth IRA, or a Keogh plan.

Property Guardian – Also known as a property manager, this is a legal adult who takes responsibility for the oversight of property inherited by a minor/child. Children under the age of 18 can inherit property, but they can only be allowed to legally own that property with adult supervision; an adult must have the responsibility of managing it.

Property Interest – This refers to the connection a person has to a specific item, piece of land, or other items.

▶ **Legal Interest** – This is property that a person can legally transfer or manage, but it is not owned by the individual. Someone who is responsible for the maintenance and oversight of the use of a piece of property but who does not legally own it is called a trustee.

▶ **Beneficial Interest** – You receive a benefit from the property.

Protective Trusts – These are designed with conditions to protect the beneficiary's property.

Provisions – Clauses that explain how you want your wishes carried out.

Q

QTIP – A qualified terminable interest property trust is a marital deduction trust, but instead of your spouse's deciding who gets the property after your death, the grantor makes that decision.

Qualified Pension Plan – A plan in which the amount of money that the employer puts into an employee's account is not taxed as income during the fiscal year the contribution is made.

R

Renter's Insurance – The exchange of premiums for a guaranteed payment to cover the loss of personal property housed in rental property that is used as a primary residence.

Revocable – A trust that can be changed.

S

Simple Will – A legal document that identifies whom you are, your beneficiaries, your executor, the directions you leave for the care of people for whom you are responsible, and the distribution of your assets.

Skimming – The act of using a special high-tech storage device to electronically "grab" account numbers and other information from a store computer register when a credit card transaction/purchase is processing.

Social Security Disability Benefit – Monthly payment made by the federal government to qualified recipients who can no longer work. Payments are made until the age of 65; at that point, you begin to receive the Social Security retirement benefit at the same rate.

Social Security Retirement Benefit – Monthly payment made by the federal government to qualified recipients who reach retirement age. Payments are based on contributions made during the individual's employment period.

Social Security Supplemental Security Income (SSI) – The federal government makes a monthly payment to qualified individuals. This benefit is for people who have little (if any) property or are blind or disabled in some other way.

Special Needs Trust – A support trust for a disabled person under the age of 65 (you or anyone else). This trust makes payments on the beneficiaries' behalf, as required by the state as reimbursement. After the beneficiary dies, the property in the trust is paid to other beneficiaries. This trust is designed to protect your property from seizure by the government or a creditor seeking reimbursement.

Special Provisions – Encompasses all clauses that create specific requirements that are unique to the beneficiary or the assets. For example, a beneficiary of a trust might be required to be 21 or graduate college before he or she can take ownership of that trust.

Spendthrift Trust – A trust that is set up for someone who will not be able to handle his or her own affairs or who is mentally incompetent, or might have financial problems and needs protection from creditors. The beneficiary does not own the property in the trust, just the payments that are made from the trust.

Spiritual Advisor – A minister, priest, monk, or some other cleric or individual trained in a specific faith tradition who offers guidance, support, and information related to their belief system.

Split-interest Trust – More than one individual benefits from the trust. One person or charity would have an interest in the trust for a specific period of time, and then another person or charity receives the property that remains.

State Estate Tax – A tax levied by the state on property left in an estate after a person dies, similar to the estate tax by the federal government, but the state tax is an additional tax burden. Not all states have an estate tax.

State Gift Tax – A tax by individual states according to terms they set that is levied against any property you give to another person or institution during a fiscal year; it can be in cash or the transfer of property, such as real estate or jewelry. Many of these are tied in some way to the federal estate tax.

State Income Tax – A tax on income earned during a fiscal year that is for residents of that state. Income earned in another state might be taxable in your state of residence, and any inheritance you receive that counts as income and is entered on your federal tax form can also be taxed.

Statutory Living Will – A legal document in which you spell out the decisions you have made about your medical care while you are still alive that complies with the statutes or laws of your state. A statutory document will likely provide more protection than a nonstatutory living will for the physicians and nurses carrying out your wishes.

Stock Bailout – The transfer of stock ownership from your name to that of a charity; the fair market value of the stock at the time of the transfer is the gift amount.

Stock Bonus Plan – A retirement plan established by an employer to give shares of the company's stock to employees. When the employee receives the shares, he or she must pay taxes based on the value of the stock.

▶   **Employee Stock Ownership Plan (ESOP)** – A retirement type of stock bonus plan. The employer contributes shares of its stock to a qualified trust, and the employee only pays taxes based on distributions she receives.

Successor Trustee – Someone who will step in if the primary trustee is unable to serve or cannot continue to manage your trust. This person will have the same legal obligations for managing the trust as the original trustee, should the successor assume the management responsibilities.

Supplemental Needs Trust – A support trust for a handicapped, elderly, or disabled person in need of support is assisted by this trust in such a way that it does not reduce or jeopardize the eligibility of that person to receive public or private benefits. This trust is designed to protect your property from seizure by the government or a creditor seeking reimbursement.

Support Trust – Requires a trustee to pay only the income and property necessary to cover the cost of education or assistance such as health care fees or nursing home fees of the beneficiaries.

Survival Clause – This leaves everything in your estate to one named person. Married people frequently do this to ensure that everything goes to the surviving spouse.

Survivor Benefit – A portion of the deceased employee's pension paid to the surviving spouse. The amount, regularly a percentage, is set by the terms of the pension plan rules.

T

Tax-deferred – The taxes on money put into an investment account are paid when it is received by the employee in the form of a distribution, not at the time the money goes into the account.

Term Insurance – A life insurance policy that carries an annual premium and pays a specified death benefit to the beneficiary but does not have a cash value, so you cannot borrow money from it. The only payment made is to the beneficiary. The death benefit is not paid if premium payments are stopped.

▶ **Annual Renewable** – A term life policy that has an annual premium and can be renewed from year to year; be sure you understand the renewal rights before signing.

▶ **Decreasing** – A term life policy in which premiums remain the same, but the benefit decreases over time. For example, if you purchase this kind of insurance (also called mortgage or credit term insurance) to pay off your debts after you die, the mortgage you want to insure might be $250,000 at the time you purchase the insurance, but the mortgage value when you die might be $150,000. The policy then pays $150,000. This kind of insurance is recommended only for those who cannot get any other kind of insurance.

▶ **Level** – A term life policy with coverage that is guaranteed for a specific period of time, or term, such as five, ten, or 20 years at a specific premium. The premium will remain for the five-year period, but at year six, it will go up and remain at that rate through the tenth year, continuing after that.

▶ **Group** – Employers frequently purchase a term life policy for each employee as an added benefit. Employees get an excellent low rate, and there is no income tax on the premiums for the first $50,000 of coverage.

Testamentary Trust – A fund created by the terms of your will after your death.

Testamentary Trust Will – This will moves your assets into one or more trusts after your death.

Testator – A person who writes a will.

Totten Trust – This is a bank account that, upon your death, immediately passes to the named beneficiary.

Trust – A legal arrangement that involves the transfer of property from the original owner to a person or a company for the purpose of holding and maintaining the property for the benefit of a specific individual, group of people, or institution(s).

Trustee – The person or company that will oversee or manage a financial resources account, such as a trust or custodian account, once it is established. This person or group will make sure the property in the trust is safe and in good order until it is turned over to the beneficiary.

Trust Agreement – The legal document that spells out the terms of a trust, including the people and conditions and the rules that must be followed; some are state or federal laws, and others are specific conditions.

Trustor – The person who sets up the trust. Other names commonly used are creator, donor, settlor, or grantor.

Trust Principal – The name given to property that is placed into a trust and is managed by a trust agreement.

U

Umbrella Liability Insurance – The exchange of premiums for a guaranteed payment to cover a host of situations that would put personal property at risk, such as personal liability or negligence.

Uniform International Wills Act – Included in the California Probate Code, to cover wills prepared out of the country.

V

Vested – To meet the predetermined requirements contained within a pension plan based on the number of years you have worked for the employer. Before an employee can receive any distributions or take full ownership of a pension plan, the employee has to be fully vested.

W

Waiver – A written statement declining the right to receive benefits signed by a spouse. This waiver must be signed to legally sever the right to claim any benefits — an alternative agreement, such as signing a prenuptial agreement, will not be enough.

Whole Life Insurance – Sometimes called cash value life insurance, this is a form of life insurance for which the insured person pays a monthly or annual premium to a company that will, upon the owner's death, pay a predetermined, fixed amount of money to the beneficiaries. A portion of the fixed (meaning it will never go up or down) premium is invested, another portion is placed into an account, like a savings account, and that cash value is accessible to the policy owner. It can be borrowed against as a loan, or the cash can be taken as the proceeds of the policy instead of the death benefit payout.

▶ **Universal Life** – A kind of whole life policy that guarantees a minimum return, but the value of the policy can go up or down. If the policy makes more money, the return might be high enough to cover your premium payments.

▶ **Joint First-to-Die or Second-to-Die** – Just as it sounds, this is a policy held by two people, and the beneficiary is paid after the first or second person dies, as designated in the policy.

Will – A legal document in which you identify what people or institutions will receive money and property from your estate after your death; it also serves to appoint guardianship of children or adults who are your legal responsibility and designates an executor to manage your estate after you die.

Will Substitute – An agreement, contract, or other legal arrangement that will accomplish the same goals of a will — to protect and transfer property rights — but without the use of a will document.

BIBLIOGRAPHY

"Advance Health Care Directive Form," Office of the Attorney General, State of California Dept. of Justice, August 22, 2008 **http://ag.ca.gov/consumers/general/adv_hc_dir.htm.**

"Animal Rights Triumph: Court Saves Sido from Mercy Killing." Tyrone Daily Herald, p. 7 (Tyrone, PA, June 18, 1980).

California Evidence Code 700, 710.

California Probate Code 100-105; 3900-3925; 4600-4605; 6110 – 6113; 1800-1804; 21620-21623.

Estate of MacLeod, 206 Cal. App. 3d 1235, 254 Cal. Rptr. 156 (1988).

"Filing Requirements for California Estate Tax Return." California State Tax Controller. **www.sco.ca.gov/ardtax_taxinfo_estate_return.html.** Accessed on November 4, 2010.

"Gift Tax." Internal Revenue Service. **www.irs.gov/businesses/small/ article/0,,id=164872,00.html.** Accessed on January 26, 2010.

Gruber, Stephen C. , Attorney. "Joint Tenancy in California." **www.ca-trusts.com/jointtenancy.html.** Accessed on November 6, 2010.

In re Estate of Wilkinson, 113 Cal. App. 645, 298 P. 1037 (1931).

In re Estate of Williams, 155 Cal. App. 4th 197, 66 Cal. Rptr. 3d 34 (2007).

"January 19, 1967 in History, Event: Herr Karl Tausch writes short-est will 'Vse Zene' (All to wife)." Brainy History. Brainymedia.com (2007). August 17, 2008 **www.brainyhistory.com/events/1967/ january_19_1967_132538.html.** Accessed on January 26, 2010.

"Majority of American Adults Remain without Wills New Lawyers.com Survey Finds." Harris Interactive. **www.harrisinteractive.com/news/news-letters/clientnews/2007_Lawyers.pdf.** Accessed on January 26, 2010.

Pender, Kathleen. (2008, July 27.) "State allows trusts to be set up for pets." **http://articles.sfgate.com/2008-07-27/business/17173744_1_pet-trusts-pet-owners-fifi-and-fido**. Accessed on November 6, 2010.

Rickard, Andrew, "This 'N' That," Advisor.ca. Advisor Group, Advisors Publishing Limited (June 2002) August, 17, 2007 **http://www.advisor. ca/freezone_nologin/article.jsp?content=20020612_000000_0000.** Accessed on January 26, 2010.

"Notice Regarding Standards for Medi-Cal Eligibility." (2010, January.) California Department of Health Care Services, Document No. DHCS 7077. **http://www.dhcs.ca.gov/formsandpubs/forms/Forms/dhcs7077.pdf.** Accessed on November 6, 2010.

U.S. Department of Labor. Bureau of Labor Statistics. **www.bls.gov.** Accessed on January 26, 2010.

"What is a Homestead? California Has Automatic Homestead Protection!" California Estate Planning Practice Blog. **http://sawdaydrake.typepad. com/estate_planning/2006/03/what_is_a_homes.html.** Accessed on November 6, 2010.

INDEX

G

Gift Tax, 76, 77, 81, 83, 120, 175, 184

Giving Clauses, 98

Golden Years, 141

Guardianship Clause, 98

H

Holographic Will, 102, 186-189, 191, 202, 203

Homestead Exemption Statute, 110

I

Incompetent, 44, 120, 188, 191

Inheritance Tax, 32, 75, 81, 138, 202

Insurance, 31, 32, 34, 37, 40, 42-44, 49, 52, 54, 62, 64, 65, 67-70, 72-74, 83, 86, 87, 105, 108, 119, 121, 125-140, 146, 148, 150-152, 167, 171, 182, 183, 215, 222, 224, 227, 229

Insurance Agent, 37, 73, 129, 133

J

Joint first-to-die or second-to-die, 135, 136

Joint Ownership, 52, 58

Joint Will, 102

K

The Keogh plan, 147

Kiddie Tax, 80

L

Life-sustaining Treatment, 106

Living Trust, 62, 68-70, 95, 120, 166, 172, 173

Living Will, 29, 67-69, 72, 101, 104-107, 204, 215, 219, 222

M

Marital-dedicational trust, 117

Medicaid, 148, 150

Medicare, 66, 148, 150, 152

Medigap insurance, 152

Minister, 38

Mutual Will, 101

N

Nest Egg, 142, 148

Non-Statutory Living Will, 276

Nuncupative Will, 104, 276

O

Opening Clauses, 97

Outright Charitable Gift, 276

Ownership, 52, 53, 56-58, 60, 62, 63, 66, 78, 97, 110, 114, 120, 122, 145, 216

P

Parchment, 60

Pension Benefit Guarantee Corporation (PBGC), 151

Pension Plan, 68, 141, 143-145, 151

Pourover Will, 277

Probate Court Judge, 51, 53

Property Guardian, 47

Property Manager, 47

Protective trust, 118, 119

Q

Qualified Terminable Interest Property trust (QTIP), 116

R

Residuary Clause, 98, 109

S

Separate Property, 58, 186

Simple Will, 97, 102, 191

Social Security Supplemental Security Income (SSI), 149

Sole Ownership, 58

Spendthrift Trust, 120

Statutory Living Will, 105

Stock Bailout, 78

Successor Trustee, 113

Survival Clause, 98

T

Testamentary Trust Will, 102

Totten Trust, 121

Trust, 22, 26, 32, 47, 48, 50, 51, 53, 57, 59, 62-64, 68-70, 72, 73, 83, 84, 95, 102, 103, 107, 111-124, 126, 133, 145, 151, 161, 166, 167, 170-174, 176, 184, 200, 201, 215, 216, 220-222, 227, 233

U

Uniform Transfer for Minors Act (UTMA), 122

Uniform Gift to Minors Act (UGMA), 122

Umbrella Liability Insurance, 133

Universal Life, 35, 136

V

Values List, 20, 24

Video Will, 104

W

Well, 11, 20, 36, 40, 44, 50, 87, 107, 147, 161, 163, 206, 220, 229, 230

Whole Life, 135, 136, 139